D1381040

# THE
# EGYPTIAN MYTHS

# THE
# EGYPTIAN MYTHS
## A GUIDE TO THE ANCIENT
## GODS AND LEGENDS

GARRY J. SHAW

WITH 95 ILLUSTRATIONS

*For Sean McKenna*

## Acknowledgments

Many thanks to Julie Patenaude for reading and commenting on the
various drafts of this book. For their support, I am also grateful to Andrew Bednarski
(Best Man!), Maggie Bryson, Henning Franzmeier, Campbell Price, the Egypt Exploration
Society, the American Research Center in Egypt and the fabulous editorial team at
Thames & Hudson. A special thanks also goes to my students at the Egypt Exploration
Society, who witnessed the 'live performance' of this book in my course, 'Gods,
Goddesses and Ghosts of the Necropolis: Mythology and Religion in Ancient Egypt'. Their
valuable comments led to many improvements throughout my developing manuscript.

*Half-title: The gods Seth (left) and Horus (right) knot lily and papyrus plants,
representing Upper and Lower Egypt respectively, around the hieroglyph for 'unity'.
Title-page: The god Anubis, a funerary deity, particularly associated with embalming,
who served as a guide to the dead.*

First published in the United Kingdom in 2014 by
Thames & Hudson Ltd, 181A High Holborn, London WC1V 7QX

First published in the United States of America in 2014 by
Thames & Hudson Inc., 500 Fifth Avenue, New York, New York 10110

Reprinted 2022

*The Egyptian Myths* © 2014 Thames & Hudson Ltd, London

British Library Cataloguing-in-Publication Data
A catalogue record for this book is available from the British Library

Library of Congress Control Number 2013948274

ISBN 978-0-500-25198-0

Printed and bound in China by Toppan Leefung Printing Limited

# CONTENTS

◄ PART THREE ►

What came before me? What is happening around me? What happens after I die? Like us today, the Egyptians sought answers to these fundamental questions and, like us, they formed theories based on observing the world around them. What we now call 'ancient Egyptian myths' was the result of these investigations; from them, a unique worldview was forged.

Mythology, more than collecting simple accounts of heroes and gods, provides a way to understand the world. There is a great ball of light in the sky; each morning it rises, spends the day crossing the sky and then it sinks in the west. What is that? And where does it go? You might ask, how does it move? Whether in the sun you see the god Re sailing across the sky aboard his day barque, or a mass of nuclear reactions pulling us around its sphere, you are observing the same phenomena. The Egyptians, trying to enhance their knowledge of the universe without recourse to particle physics, simply came to different conclusions. Their explanations fuelled their distinctive outlook and shaped their experience; myth became

The hawk-headed Re sails aboard his solar barque.

Horus the Child, son of Osiris and Isis.

the backbone of society, a culture-wide filter for an impassive reality. Once immersed in the internal logic of its ideology, life made more sense; order took the place of disorder; control replaced helplessness; knowledge overcame ignorance. The world, with its violent desert storms and deadly scorpions, became a little less frightening.

The mythic narrative of ancient Egypt was ever-present in people's lives – it played out over the course of each day as an endless repetition of creations, destructions and rebirths, entangled in a net of divine interactions. There was no need to set these events as an immutable narrative. Each person lived as the hero of their own mythic narrative each day. Gods, as personalized forces, were present in every facet of the created world and mythic precedents could be cited as explanations for both extraordinary and mundane events, linking the individual to the world of the gods. Moreover, by invoking mythic events, the Egyptians assimilated themselves with their deities. A person with a headache became Horus the Child, cared for by his mother, who herself became Isis; in death, the deceased transformed into various gods whilst traversing the afterlife realm, assuming each deity's divine authority for a time. Egypt's myths were elastic enough to be shaped into everyone's lives, as each individual sought to explain the natural world and the challenges and joys of existence. Myths, and the acts of the gods detailed therein, answered the question, 'why did this happen to me?' There is comfort in precedent.

◄ RECONSTRUCTING EGYPTIAN MYTHOLOGY ►

Today, Egyptologists are faced with scattered and fragmentary references to Egypt's myths, assembled from the content of disparate sources dating from 3050 BC through to the first centuries AD. As can be seen, the time span covered by 'ancient Egypt' is extremely long, over 3,000 years depending on where the lines are drawn. Owing to the difficulty of assigning specific dates to events, Egyptologists tend

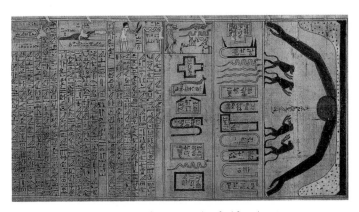

The mounds of the Duat – the afterlife realm.

not to cite dates BC, and instead refer to the reign of the king, his dynasty or the general period in which he ruled. In the 3rd century BC, the Egyptian priest Manetho divided Egypt's kings into 30 dynasties (later writers added a 31st). Though each dynasty implies a distinct ruling line – an individual bloodline – this is not always the case, as Manetho also used significant events, such as the construction of the first pyramid or a change of royal residence, to draw the line between phases. Modern Egyptologists took Manetho's dynasties and grouped them into longer phases, divided between periods when there was a single king ruling over the entire country (Early Dynastic Period, Old Kingdom, Middle Kingdom, New Kingdom, Late Period) and when the kingship was divided (First Intermediate Period, Second Intermediate Period, Third Intermediate Period). These major phases of 'the Pharaonic Period' were followed by the Ptolemaic Period, when kings of Macedonian-Greek origin ruled, and afterwards the Roman Period. In this book, I have followed these Egyptological dating conventions.

**Egyptian Chronology**

| | | | |
|---|---|---|---|
| Pharaonic Period | Early Dynastic Period | c. 3050–2660 BC | Dynasties 1–2 |
| | Old Kingdom | c. 2660–2190 BC | Dynasties 3–6 |
| | First Intermediate Period | c. 2190–2066 BC | Dynasties 7–11 |
| | Middle Kingdom | c. 2066–1780 BC | Dynasties 11–12 |
| | Second Intermediate Period | c. 1780–1549 BC | Dynasties 13–17 |
| | New Kingdom | c. 1549–1069 BC | Dynasties 18–20 |
| | Third Intermediate Period | c. 1069–664 BC | Dynasties 21–25 |
| | Late Period | 664–332 BC | Dynasties 26–31 |
| | Ptolemaic Period | 332–30 BC | |
| | Roman Period | 30 BC–AD 395 | |

**The Two Lands**

Egypt is a land of stark contrasts: flowing from south to north, the river Nile snakes its way through the Nile Valley, flanked by a narrow band of cultivable land, until it reaches ancient Memphis, near modern Cairo, where it fans out as a series of tributaries to form the great fertile triangle of the Delta. Owing to this dramatic change in terrain, the Egyptians divided their country into Upper (southern) and Lower (northern) Egypt – the Nile Valley south of Memphis and the Delta respectively – and referred to it as the Two Lands. A different crown represented each half – the Red Crown for Lower Egypt and the White Crown for Upper Egypt; these were combined as the Double Crown, representative of the king's dominion over the whole country. Similarly, the Egyptians were struck by the strong contrast between the barren dry desert, which they referred to as the 'red land', and the cultivable soil, called the 'black land'. East and west also had significance; watching the rising sun, the Egyptians came to associate the east with new life and rebirth, while the west, where the sun 'died' each evening, became the realm of the dead; this is why cemeteries were often built in the desert on the west side of the Nile.

As there is no single source that neatly explains to us the myths of the ancient Egyptians, Egyptologists are forced to piece them together from the already fragmentary evidence that survives from those distant times. Many myths were recorded on papyri, discovered within burials or at temple sites; others are alluded to on funerary stelae placed in tombs. The modern names given to some sources reflect their original contexts: the Pyramid Texts were found inscribed on the walls of Old Kingdom royal pyramids from the end of the 5th Dynasty onwards, while the Coffin Texts, known from the Middle Kingdom, were painted onto coffins used to bury those who could afford such luxuries. The Book of the Dead ('The Book of Coming Forth by Day' to the Egyptians), copied onto papyrus rolls and coffins, provided the deceased with a travel guide to the

The Greek historian Plutarch recorded many Egyptian myths.

afterlife from the late Second Intermediate Period, and was in use for over a thousand years beyond that time. In almost all cases, the myths are abbreviated or mentioned only cryptically; sometimes this was due to decorum – the Egyptians shy away from referring to the death of Osiris within their funerary monuments, for example, as the description of this traumatic event in a tomb context could magically harm the deceased – while in other cases, there was no need to explain the myth in full, as it was assumed that the reader would already know the story.

Over the vast span of Egyptian history, Egypt was influenced by cultures throughout the Eastern Mediterranean and Near Eastern World – in certain periods it was even ruled by them, from the Assyrians and Persians, to the Macedonian-Greeks and Romans. Egypt's myths adapted with their times, soaking up new flavours and finding new expression thanks to these influences. Variations on myths also developed in each Egyptian province (called 'nomes'); there was thus no single, correct version. This is both distressing and liberating; distressing because any guide to Egyptian myth can never be a true reflection of what the Egyptians believed; but liberating because, as its chronicler, I am not fixed to a rigid retelling. What follows in this book is more akin to the work of Plutarch, who took the elements of the Osiris myth and pieced them together for a Greek audience, than a typical academic analysis. Like Plutarch, in places, I have taken mythic fragments, sometimes from different time periods, and created a coherent narrative; if the reader can forgive Plutarch for such acts of 'cherry picking', I am hopeful that I too may be forgiven.

◄ UNDERSTANDING THE GODS ►

The Egyptian gods are a vibrant and eclectic group; they squabble, fight, murder, form relationships and can die of old age (before being reborn, illustrative of the Egyptian love of cyclical time). They could also manifest in a variety of forms, in various locations simultaneously, whilst their true selves remained distant and invisible in the sky; though malleable in form, they were, nevertheless, neither omniscient nor omnipresent. Charged with specific divine responsibilities (Osiris for regeneration, Min for fertility, for example), they were restricted in their powers, and had to merge with each other to share each other's powers for a short time, if they needed to achieve a goal beyond their cosmic remit: thus, lacking the ability and power to re-energize himself, the ailing sun god merges with Osiris each night, using this god's regenerative force to enable him to be born again in a new dawn. Sometimes, when one god assumed the characteristics of another, (s)he transformed into that other deity; so, when Hathor, as Eye of Re, attacked mankind, her violent rage transformed her into the overtly bloodthirsty goddess Sekhmet. Though initially confusing to modern readers, the complex nature of Egypt's gods should become clearer as the following pages turn.

It must be noted that, although useful, detailed analyses of the gods' development and assorted cults over time distract from their character, and as such, have been largely omitted from this book in favour of stressing their personalities and 'human' characteristics. For those readers or students new to ancient Egypt, or those with only a casual interest, I am hopeful that my approach will be beneficial, providing a useful introduction to the myths, allowing the stories to breathe with only a limited amount of modern, analytical intrusion. Above all else, reading these myths and learning about how the Egyptians engaged with the world through them, should be enjoyable: as well as being explanatory, myths were meant to entertain. It is in this spirit that I hope the reader will approach this book.

To address the questions posed at the start of this introduction, I have divided this book into three parts: 1) The Time of the Gods (Or Explaining Where We All Came from); 2) The Living World (Or Explaining the World around Us); and 3) The Mythology of Death (Or Explaining the Life Hereafter). As you read on, my hope is that you will place yourself into the sandals of an ancient Egyptian and try to see the world from his or her perspective. Take these mythic explanations and imagine what it was like to see, and understand, the world in this way. These myths are insights into ancient psychology, windows into the Egyptian mind, and can introduce you to a whole new – yet simultaneously old – way of experiencing the world.

# PART ONE

~~~~~~~~~~

## THE TIME OF THE GODS
(OR EXPLAINING
WHERE
WE ALL CAME FROM)

◄ O ►

## DISORDER AND CREATION

Understanding ancient Egyptian thought on creation, or indeed reconstructing Egyptian myth overall, is like trying to piece together a jigsaw puzzle when the majority of the pieces are missing and someone has thrown away the box.

In the past, faced with scattered, diverse and apparently contradictory remnants of creation myths from different parts of the country, Egyptologists divided these mythic snippets according to the cult centre that they assumed had produced (or standardized) the source material – scholarship on these would refer to 'the Memphite Theology' (from the city of Memphis) or 'the Heliopolitan Theology' (from Heliopolis). Sometimes it was argued that these cult centres, with their various interpretations, were 'competing', implying that Egypt's priests snubbed their noses at their counterparts in different cities because one might prioritize the god Amun in his guise as 'the Great Honker' over the divine cow that engendered Re.

Perhaps they did. But whatever the case may be, these various creation accounts, in actuality, display remarkable cohesion, exhibiting the same fundamental themes and following similar structures. The regional cult centres, it seems, put their own spin on generally agreed mythological essentials, emphasizing the roles of particular actors, phases or aspects of creation, and substituting their own local gods for those mentioned in other versions. In this way, Egypt's various priesthoods put forward alternative, rather than competing, views, thereby reducing the risk of inter-faith fisticuffs.

So, although no universally followed creation myth existed, there was, at least, an overarching concept – a shared foundation – for how creation generally occurred: deep within Nun (the limitless dark ocean) a god awakened, or conceived of creation. Through his power, he, or his manifestations, divided into the many aspects of the created world, creating the first gods and the first mound of earth to emerge from the water. Afterwards, the sun – in some accounts the independent eye of the creator, in others, newly hatched from an egg – dawned for the first time, bringing light to where once had been darkness.

The god Nun raises the solar barque into the sky.

The Hermopolitan Ogdoad flank the solar barque: four on each side.

During the New Kingdom, in about 1200 BC, there was an attempt at Thebes to unify Egypt's main traditions under the god Amun as ultimate creator. This period is, therefore, a perfect standpoint from which to describe creation in more detail, as its texts provide the best insight into the Egyptian conception of where the world came from, while also incorporating the preferred traditions of the country's most important cult centres – predominantly those of Hermopolis, which focused on the eight gods (Ogdoad) of the pre-creation universe (see below); of the god Ptah's temple at Memphis, in which the spoken word brought all things into existence; and of Heliopolis, in which the god (Re-)Atum evolved from a single egg or seed into the physical world. Thus, in this chapter, drawing on the work of Egyptologist James P. Allen, and guided by quotations from the Ramesside Great Hymn to Amun – a unique text that presents the conclusions of the Amun priesthood's theological explorations – we will investigate the creation of the world.

◄ THE CREATORS ►

### Nun – The Infinite Waters

The pre-creation universe is an infinite body of water, an expanse of darkness, inert and motionless; a place to bring a submarine rather than a spaceship. There is no separation of the elements,

The shape of this pyramidion probably represents the first mound of creation.

no earth and sky, nothing is named, and there is no death or life. It has existed in this form for all eternity, unending, still, silent. Though beyond true human comprehension, to conceptualize and discuss this infinite watery expanse, the Egyptians personified its intertwined aspects as indissoluble male and female couples – the males as frogs and the females as snakes. There was Nun and Naunet as the limitless waters; Huh and Hauhet as infinity; Kuk and Kauket as darkness; and Amun and Amunet as hiddenness. These forces are often collectively referred to as the eight primeval gods of Hermopolis, or the Ogdoad (from the Greek for 'eight').

To the theologians of Hermopolis, who emphasized these forces of pre-creation in their myths, the eight gods created the first mound of earth (or island) together, and then formed an egg from which the sun god hatched. Depending on the myth at hand, sometimes the sun is said to hatch from an egg laid by a goose called the Great Honker, or by the god Thoth (see p. 51) in the form of an ibis. In other variations, the eight gods create a lotus in Nun, from which the sun is born, first taking the form of the scarab beetle Khepri and then as the child-god Nefertum whose eyes, when open, gave light to the world.

Of the eight aspects of the pre-created universe, Nun, as the limitless waters, was of particular importance. Though sometimes depicted like his male companions as a frog, he could also be shown as a human with a tripartite wig, or as a fecundity figure, representing bounty, fruitfulness and fertility, for, as we shall see, though Nun was inert and motionless, dark and infinite, he was also generative – a place of birth and possibility. This might seem counterintuitive: how can a place of darkness and disorder be a force for growth and life? As an optimistic civilization, the Egyptians saw in Nun potential for being and regeneration: light comes from darkness, land emerges from floodwater with renewed fertility, flowers grow from dry, lifeless seeds. The potential for order existed within disorder.

It is from within Nun that all things began.

### Amun 'Who Made Himself into Millions'

*The Eight were your [Amun's] first form...*
*Another of his [Amun's] forms is the Ogdoad...*
THE GREAT HYMN TO AMUN

Amun, listed above as just one of the eight primeval gods, was by 1200 BC of unparalleled importance in Egyptian state religion, so much so that the Ogdoad of Hermopolis was now regarded as the first development of his own majestic hidden power. The Egyptians depicted Amun as a man with blue skin, wearing a crown of two tall feathered plumes. His title 'the Great Honker' demonstrates his

King Seti I (right) bows his head to the god Amun-Re.

association with the goose, the bird who broke the silence at the beginning of time with his honking; and he could also be shown as a ram – a symbol of fertility. Although Amun's divine wife was normally said to be Mut (see box opposite), as one of the primeval forces of Nun, he found his female counterpart in Amunet (who is sometimes shown wearing the crown of Lower Egypt and carrying a papyrus-headed staff).

In the Middle Kingdom (2066–1780 BC), Amun rose to prominence in the Theban region, and in the New Kingdom (1549–1069 BC) reigned supreme as ultimate deity, referred to as King of the Gods. Representing all that was hidden, Amun existed within and beyond Nun, transcendent, invisible, behind all things, in existence before the gods of creation, and self-created. He 'knit his fluid

## The Gods of Creation

### The Ogdoad of Hermopolis

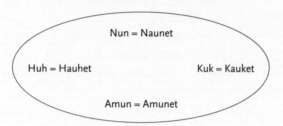

Nun = Naunet

Huh = Hauhet          Kuk = Kauket

Amun = Amunet

### The Theban triad

Amun  =  Mut

|

Khonsu

### The Memphite triad

Ptah(-Tatenen) = Sekhmet

|

Nefertum

### The Ennead of Heliopolis, with Horus

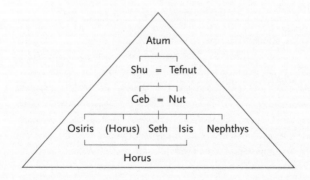

Atum

Shu  =  Tefnut

Geb  =  Nut

Osiris  (Horus)  Seth  Isis  Nephthys

Horus

together with his body to bring about his egg in isolation', we are told, and was 'creator of his [own] perfection'. Even the gods did not know his true character.

*He [Amun] is hidden from the gods, and his aspect*
*is unknown. He is farther than the sky,*
*he is deeper that the Duat [the afterlife realm].*
*No god knows his true appearance,*
*no processional image of his is unfolded through inscriptions,*
*no one testifies to him accurately.*
THE GREAT HYMN TO AMUN

Amun's inaccessibility is probably a good thing, as we are also informed that anyone who 'expresses his secret identity, unknowingly or knowingly', would instantly drop down dead.

Simultaneously within and beyond Nun, Amun, the ultimate hidden deity, decided to create the world:

*He began speaking in the midst of silence…*
*He began crying out while the world was in stillness,*
*his yell in circulation while he had no second, that*
*he might give birth to what is and cause them to live…*
THE GREAT HYMN TO AMUN

**Amun, Mut and Khonsu: The Theban Triad**
According to Theban theology, Amun's wife was the goddess Mut. She was depicted predominantly in human form, but also as a lioness. Mut was a divine female pharaoh, and served as a mother goddess; consequently, she can be shown wearing the Double Crown of Upper and Lower Egypt, and a vulture headdress, associated with goddesses and queens. Amun and Mut's trinity was completed with their son, Khonsu, depicted as a child with full and crescent moons together upon his head (see also pp. 122–23).

## Ptah – The Creative Mind

> *You took your [next] form as [Ptah]-Tatenen…*
> *He [Amun] is called [Ptah]-Tatenen…*
> THE GREAT HYMN TO AMUN

Amun's straightforward, intellectual act of thinking and speaking required the intervention of another god: Ptah, god of arts and crafts, the divine sculptor and the power of the creative mind. To the priests of Ptah, all things were a 'creation of his heart': whether deities, the sky, the land, art or technology, each was conceived of and spoken into existence by their god. Worshipped primarily at Memphis, near modern Cairo, Ptah was shown as a man tightly wrapped in cloth like a mummy, standing on a pedestal, gripping a sceptre, wearing a skull cap and with a straight beard (unusual for a god, as they normally preferred curving beards). He formed a family triad with the volatile lion goddess Sekhmet, and their son Nefertum, depicted as a child with a lotus flower on his head.

The god Ptah.

The god Tatenen.

### Sekhmet

The goddess Sekhmet, meaning 'powerful', was depicted as a lion-headed woman, with a long wig and solar disc upon her head. Rarely, she was shown fully as a lioness. She was wife of the god Ptah, and mother of Nefertum.

Sekhmet could be either a dangerous or protective force. She was associated with plagues (brought by the messengers of Sekhmet), warfare and aggression, but was also prayed to for protection from disease; if a person became sick, he could summon priests of Sekhmet, and ask them to use their knowledge of magic to cure his illness. Sekhmet also served as a protector to the king, breathing fire at his enemies and accompanying him during warfare. In her manifestation as the bloodthirsty Eye of Re, Sekhmet attempted to destroy mankind, but was tricked into halting her rampage (see pp. 58–59). Her main cult centre was at Memphis.

From the Ramesside Period, when the Great Hymn to Amun was composed, the god Tatenen ('the risen land') was regarded as a manifestation of Ptah; consequently, the two were united as Ptah-Tatenen, a combination of divine sculptor and the first land to rise from the waters of Nun.

As the power of the creative mind, Ptah represented the transformative force that turns a creative thought into action and material reality – from the flash of inspiration that a craftsman might suddenly experience in his mind while strolling down the street, to the act of physically carving his statue, manipulating the stone into the image he had perceived in his mind's eye. This is reflected in a text known as the Memphite Theology, which is normally interpreted as stating that creation occurred through the heart and tongue of Ptah, this god conceiving of the elements of creation in his heart, and announcing them into existence with his divine words as he pronounced their names: whatever he thought became real. It was creation *ex nihilo*. However, James P. Allen has recently argued that the heart and tongue in question in fact belong to the ultimate creator, Amun, with Ptah simply supplying the transformative force. So, the priests of Amun might have admitted, although Amun spoke 'in the midst of silence', this hidden god providing the vision of creation, it was Ptah, as personification of the creative process, who enabled Amun's thoughts to be realized.

### Hu, Sia and Heka

The intellectual act of creation was possible because of three facets of the creator, his *sia* 'divine perception', *hu* 'authoritative utterance' and *heka* 'magic'. With the power of *heka*, he perceived the created world in his heart, and through his authoritative utterance spoke it into existence. Each of these three forces was personified as an individual god, with Hu and Sia said to come into being from drops of blood dripped from the phallus of the sun god.

*Heka*, however, came into existence, 'before two things had developed in the world', and thus, when personified, is sometimes presented as a creator god. Illustrated as a man or sometimes as a child, Heka often sports a curved divine beard. The hindquarters of a lion can be shown atop his head, and he sometimes holds snakes in his hands. He is one of the select deities that protect the sun god as he travels in his solar barque, but similarly protects the god Osiris in the afterlife realm of the Duat.

The gods Sia (left) and Heka (right) flank the ram-headed soul of the sun god.

If, then, we imagine Amun as a wealthy benefactor, a man commissioning a statue to his particular requirements, and Ptah as the divine artist and craftsman hired to realize this work, what, or who, was the raw material upon which Amun, as ultimate creator, and Ptah, as translator of the creator's will, were to work? Who or what were they to affect with their actions? Every artisan requires a substance to mould, to enable him to extract his vision from his mind and make the abstract concrete for all to see. In Egyptian creation mythology, this raw material was the god Atum (or Re-Atum), 'sculpted' into the created world we all exist within.

## Atum and Physical Evolution

*He [Amun] completed himself as Atum,*
*being of one body with him.*
THE GREAT HYMN TO AMUN

These intellectual acts – the vision of Amun and the creative force of Ptah – set the physical evolution of the world in motion, acting upon and stirring into consciousness an egg or seed floating in the limitless and dark expanse of Nun. In the Heliopolitan tradition, this seed was the god Atum (also referred to as Re-Atum). At this point a fusion of all matter and gods, mixed together and undifferentiated, Atum was like the singularity at the start of the big bang or, as he himself relates:

*I was alone with the Primeval Ocean [Nun] in the inertness, and*
*could find no place to stand ... [the gods of the] first generation*
*had not yet come into being, [but] they were with me...*
COFFIN TEXT 80

Atum, meaning 'the finisher', was the Lord of Totality, a god that simultaneously represented evolution and the completion of evolution. Typically depicted in human form, wearing the Double Crown of Upper and Lower Egypt, Atum could also take the form of

The god Atum (left) sits before Queen Nefertari.

a mongoose, scarab beetle, lizard, snake, a bow-and-arrow wielding baboon or the *benu*-bird; he is also sometimes depicted as the first land to emerge from the waters during creation. As the evening form of the sun god, he was shown with a ram's head.

Within Nun, Atum (still only a seed) began a conversation with the limitless expanse of Nun:

> *I am floating, being entirely numb, totally inert.*
> *It is my son, "Life" [here, the god Shu], who will constitute*
> *my consciousness, who will make my heart live…*
> COFFIN TEXT 80

Nun responded:

> *Inhale your daughter Maat [here, a form of the goddess Tefnut]*
> *and raise her to your nostril so that your consciousness may live.*
> *May they not be far from you, your daughter Maat and*
> *your son Shu, whose name is "Life"… it is your son Shu who*
> *will lift you up.*
> COFFIN TEXT 80

This curious first conversation ever held requires explanation. At this point in creation, the gods Shu and Tefnut, representing life and the concept of *maat* (see box opposite), are within Atum, existing as part of him. In order for Atum to separate himself from the infinite waters and enjoy an independent existence, 'life' takes position as his consciousness, initiating his heartbeat, as if resuscitating him from death. His heart beating and his mind now active, Atum, nevertheless, remains unconscious until he inhales Maat/Tefnut, taking her into his body as the breath of life to awaken him to full consciousness. As if passing from death into a coma and then awakening from that dream-like state, Atum becomes fully conscious and able to act, roused from his dormant, inert state by the power of breath, heartbeat and mind.

Now fully in control of his actions, Atum takes advantage of his independence to 'subtract' the waters of Nun from him and become 'the remainder' – this, the first significant matter in the universe,

The goddess Tefnut.

The god Shu.

## Maat and Isfet

*Maat*, whether as a goddess, a concept or indeed as a form of Tefnut, plays a key role in the Egyptian conception of the universe. As a concept, *maat* represented the correct balance between order and disorder, while also encompassing justice and right action. The Egyptians acknowledged that disorder (*isfet*) could never be eradicated, nor should it be, for it was part of creation, necessary to its correct functioning. *Isfet* had been an integral part of the cosmos since the beginning of time.

It was, however, not made by the creator, and he dissociated himself from the *isfet* performed by humans:

> *I made every man like his fellow, I did not command that they do isfet: it is their hearts that destroy what I have laid out.*
>
> COFFIN TEXT 1160

The aim of every living being, from the gods to the pharaoh and mankind, was to ensure that order (*maat*) was not overtaken by disorder (*isfet*). To the Egyptians, *maat* permeated all things, and those who broke its laws were punished, whether they knew of them or not. The gods even lived on *maat*, referring to it as their beer, food and drink. When personified, Maat was a goddess wearing a tall feather on her head – the hieroglyphic symbol for *maat*. Perhaps due to her connection with Tefnut, Maat is cited as a daughter of Re(-Atum), and is sometimes described as the consort of the god Thoth.

The goddess Maat.

represented by the Egyptians as the mound of creation (itself personified as the god Tatenen), was perhaps the inspiration behind the pyramid form; in variations of the creation myth, the sacred *benu*-bird, an aspect of Atum, arrives to perch on this mound and its cry is the first sound in existence.

Returning to our narrative, the god Shu, within Atum, now expands, as if Atum is a balloon filling with air:

> *It is in the body of the great self-developing god [Atum] that*
> *I have developed… It is in his feet that I have grown, in his arms*
> *that I have developed, in his limbs that I have made a void.*
> COFFIN TEXT 75

Atum now evolves into the created world, taking form as he desires. This self-creating power is frequently celebrated in Egyptian spells:

> *It was through my [Atum's] effectiveness that I brought*
> *about my body. I am the one who made me. It was*
> *as I wished, according to my heart, that I built myself.*
> COFFIN TEXT 714

> *Hail Atum! – who made the sky, who created what exists;*
> *who emerged as land, who created seed; lord of what*
> *is, who gave birth to the gods; great god, self-developing.*
> BOOK OF THE DEAD, SPELL 79

◄ THE CREATED ►

**The First Generation of Gods**
Shu and Tefnut now become separate from Atum, ejected from his body as divine fluid through his sneezing, spitting or masturbating, depending on the variant of the myth. They remain within the confines of his expanding shape, stuck in the 'balloon' of the created world. However, despite now being detached, Shu and Tefnut each

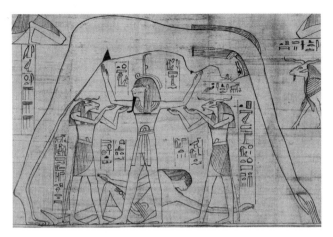

Shu (centre), arms raised, separates Nut as the sky, from Geb, lying below as the earth.

lack their own life force, remaining dependent on their creator for their survival. To remedy this, just as they, in the form of 'life' and Maat, had given Atum the power necessary to separate from Nun, Atum now embraces his twin children and passes his *ka* or 'life force' to them, allowing them full freedom of movement and existence.

As an independent god, Tefnut is sometimes depicted as a human woman, but is most often shown as a lioness with a human body. Her role in the created world is rather uncertain; Egyptologists refer to her as 'moisture' or 'corrosive moist air', or believe that she served as the upper limit of the Duat – the afterlife realm. For certain, however, she acted as the mother of all future gods.

Shu, on the other hand, is easier to describe. Typically shown as a man with a feather on his head, he could also be depicted as a lion, in the same manner as his sister/wife. In illustrations of the cosmos, he stands with his arms raised, separating the sky from the earth in his role as the atmosphere. Like a void within a sealed cave, Shu acted as a dry and empty space within the confines of the created world of Atum – delineating the firm limits of our existence. Creating and ensuring the separation between above and below, Shu formed the space in which all life and movement could now exist.

The creation of a space in which all life could thrive was not the only result of Shu and Tefnut's separation from Atum: time also came into being. Shu represented *neheh*, the Egyptian concept of cyclical time, or never-ending recurrence, such as the rising and setting sun, the annual inundation, the cycle of birth and death, growth and decay. Tefnut, on the other hand, was *djet*, meaning time at a standstill, covering everything that is remaining and lasting, such as mummies or stone architecture.

With physical and temporal space now in existence, the scene was set for the first sunrise and the creation of mankind.

### The Sole Eye of Atum and the First Sunrise

Shu and Tefnut were nurtured in the waters of Nun – regarded as a generative and regenerative force owing to its role in creation. There, they were overseen by Atum's Sole Eye, who was sent out to follow, or to go in search of, the twin children by their father. The Eye of Atum (more often referred to as the Eye of Re due to the close association between these two gods, see Chapter 2) is a recurrent character in Egyptian mythology. As well as representing the solar disc, the god's eye could represent the moon or the morning star, depending on the myth at hand. It acts independently of his whole, and, in this separate form, appears as a manifestation of a goddess – often Hathor, Bastet or Mut (see boxes pp. 58, 35 and 24). By sending out his Sole Eye to search for Shu and Tefnut, Atum initiated the first sunrise. This in itself would not have been possible without Shu creating a void. For this reason, Shu says, 'I made light of the darkness', and 'it is I who make the sky light after Darkness'. Still, despite the Sole Eye appearing as a goddess and being separate from Atum, the solar disc nevertheless remained part of him; the sun was still 'Atum in his disc' or Atum who 'goes forth from the eastern horizon' or, more succinctly, Re-Atum – the visible sign of the creator's power (for Re was the name of the sun (god) at his most powerful at midday, and Atum his name in the evening, when in old age, see Chapter 2). (Re-)Atum now began his daily journey across the sky, and passed through the afterlife realm of the Duat at night (see Chapter 5).

---

**Bastet**

At first depicted as a lioness, and later as a cat or cat-headed woman, often holding a sistrum decorated with cats, Bastet (probably meaning 'She of the Ointment Jar') acted as a divine mother and nurse to the king. She was also associated with female fertility, and provided protection to pregnant women, as well as the deceased. As the 'Cat of Re' she destroyed the chaos snake Apophis, and, like many goddesses, was associated with the Eye of Re, leading to her being described as his daughter. Bastet's cult centre was at Bubastis (Tell Basta) in the Delta, and she was the mother of the god Mahes, who was shown as a lion or lion-headed man.

---

## Mankind

According to one myth, when the time came for Shu, Tefnut and the Eye to return to Atum, the Eye was shocked to discover that she had been replaced with a new solar eye, called 'the Glorious One'. The unwanted eye became so angry that she cried in rage; her tears created humanity. To soothe her pain, Atum placed her on his forehead, where she 'exercised governance over the entire land'. It seems that she transformed into a *uraeus* – a rearing cobra, worn by all pharaohs, that spits fire at the enemies of order.

Similar myths provide variant tales of the origin of mankind. In one, people are said to be the result of the 'blindness that is behind the god', suggesting that the Eye cried so much that she lost her sight, while in Coffin Text 80, Atum refers to human beings as having come forth from his Eye. Another myth presents the sun god weeping because he is alone after his birth and unable to find his mother; these tears created mankind. The gods themselves, on the other hand, are described as springing from the sun god's smile, or as emerging from the creator's sweat (this is not as derogatory as it may at first seem, as a god's sweat was believed to smell of incense).

Despite mankind being an accidental consequence of the Eye's despair, anger and sadness, the creator performed four good deeds for their benefit. He created the four winds to give the 'breath of life' to everybody; he made the annual Nile flood to ensure that there would always be enough food; everyone was created equal (other than the king, naturally, who existed in his own category); and he made every person's heart remember the 'West' – the afterlife. There, they could continue their existence in the company of the gods. Indeed, the creator was not indifferent to his accidental creation:

> For it is for their sake that He created heaven and earth.
> He stilled the raging of the waters, and created the winds so
> that their nostrils might live. They are His images who come forth
> from His body, and it is for their sake that He rises in the sky.
> For them He created plants and cattle, fowl and fish to sustain
> them… For their sake He creates the daylight… And when
> they weep, He hearkens… [It is He] who watches over them
> by night as by day.
> THE TEACHING FOR KING MERIKARE

Additionally, a hymn to Amun elucidates what this god did for the world's non-human population, stating that he was 'creator of pasture that keeps the animals alive … who makes it possible for the fish in the river to live and the birds to populate the air'. Amun even cares for the smallest of creatures, the hymn relates, for it is he 'who makes it all possible for the mosquitoes to live together with the worms and fleas, who takes care of the mice in their holes, and keeps alive the beetles (?) in every tree…'.

The god Atum fights the chaos snake Apophis.

## Apophis and His Origins

Each night, from the moment of creation, Apophis, a monstrous snake, 120 cubits (about 63m or 206ft) long, who represented disorder, attacked the sun god and fostered rebellion. As the ultimate destructive force in the universe, Apophis was leader of the forces of disorder and had to be repelled from the sun god Re's solar barque by his followers in order to ensure the sunrise and the continued stability of the world. Described as 'the Roarer' and lacking nose, ears and eyes, Apophis nevertheless still managed to possess the Evil Eye, which gave him the ability to paralyse men and gods. For this reason, kings performed a ritual in which they struck the Eye of Apophis with a bat, flinging away his evil gaze.

Despite Apophis' prominent role in Egyptian mythology, his origins are rather shadowy. There is only one late reference to his creation. In this, he comes into existence from the discarded spittle of Neith. For most of Egyptian history, however, there is no reference to Apophis coming into being, as if he were regarded as somehow self-created or in existence before creation.

---

**Apophis: Still Out to Get Us**

Unlike the snake Apophis, who threatened to destroy the sun each day, the asteroid named Apophis represents an intermittent danger to the Earth and Moon. As you'll be happy to learn, the predicted 2004 Earth impact did not in fact happen, but calculations made soon after that (non-)event showed that impacts were also possible in 2029 and 2036; luckily, both have since been discounted as extremely unlikely. Interestingly, the asteroid was named Apophis not because of its danger to the survival of the world, but because its discoverers were fans of the television series Stargate SG1, which included a character named Apophis as the main villain.

---

## The Next Generation

Shu and Tefnut engendered the next generation of gods: Geb and Nut. As a force, Nut served as the sky vault, a transparent barrier between the created world and the surrounding waters of Nun, stopping them from crashing down upon the earth. Personified, she is most often depicted as a naked woman, holding herself up by her arms and legs, which are either to be envisioned as making contact with the earth at the cardinal points, or as held closely together, causing her body to be a thin path for the sun, moon, and stars to travel along. Quite unusually for Egyptian art, Nut can also be portrayed face-on, looking directly at the viewer, as if you are gazing up into the sky and seeing her staring down at you from on high.

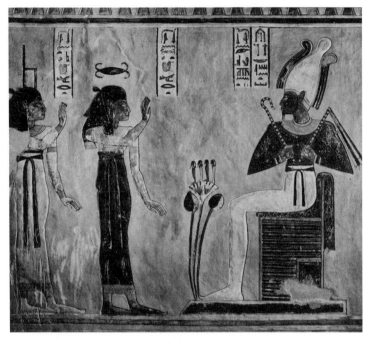

The goddess Neith (centre) stands between Isis and the enthroned Osiris.

Geb, the god who became the earth, is normally personified as a human with green skin, sometimes decorated with plants, lying on his side and leaning on his elbow. When standing, he often wears the Red Crown of Lower Egypt, though this is sometimes replaced by a goose – the hieroglyphic symbol of his name.

One myth tells us that at first Geb and Nut embraced each other so closely that Nut was unable to give birth, but Shu forced them apart to allow her children to be born; this neatly explains why the atmosphere separates the earth from the sky. In another myth, presented by the Greek historian Plutarch, Geb and Nut were unable to sleep together because Shu held them apart, forcing them to meet in secret. Re, however, discovered their secret liaisons and placed a

The god Geb.

curse on Nut, rendering her incapable of giving birth 360 days of the year – the whole of the year at this early point in creation. The wise god Thoth (whose technical lack of existence in creation at this point we'll quietly ignore for the moment) offered to help and went to play draughts with the moon. As good at gambling as he is at scribal practice (see p. 51), Thoth defeated the moon and won 'the seventieth part of each of her illuminations'. From this he composed five days to add to the end of the year, taking the calendar to 365 days, and allowing Nut the chance to give birth to her children; this she did on each of these five days.

The children of Nut and Geb, in the order in which they were born, are: Osiris, Horus the Elder, Seth (breaking through his mother's side), Isis and Nephthys. In non-Greek sources, Horus the Elder is typically omitted, leaving us with Egypt's traditional Great Ennead – the group of nine gods who represented the physical creation of the world (see box p. 23).

◄ CREATION COMPLETE ►

*The Ennead is combined in your [Amun's] body:*
*your image is every god, joined in your person.*
*You emerged first, you began from the start.*
THE GREAT HYMN TO AMUN

And so, the priests of Amun might have told you, what began with Amun yelling in the midst of silence culminated with the evolution of the physical world; he is the 'original one who begot the

Members of the Heliopolitan Ennead (Atum, Shu, Tefnut, Geb, Nut and (side by side) Isis and Nephthys) followed by Horus and Hathor. Re-Horakhety is at their head. Osiris and Seth are missing.

original ones and caused the sun to be born, completing himself in Atum, one body with him'. Creation was a result of the actions of Amun, and each development in the world after that moment was a development of him. Similarly, every facet of the universe is a manifestation of his hidden force, acting as independent forces and personalities, permeating all existence within our bubble of creation, but all interlocking and unified.

These forces are the *netjeru,* 'the gods'.

# THE REIGNS OF KINGS RE, SHU AND GEB

Before men were kings of Egypt, the gods themselves reigned and lived among humanity. The first of these is sometimes said to be Ptah, but no myth tells us about his reign. His name was added to the Turin King List, which is one of our main sources for the order of Egyptian kings' reigns, going far back into early history, even to include the gods themselves; however, the inclusion of Ptah's name at the head of this list may reflect only a local tradition. More widely acclaimed as the first king of Egypt was the sun god, Re(-Atum).

## ◄ THE REIGN OF KING RE ►

As one of Egypt's most important deities, Re was worshipped throughout the country, though his main cult centre was at Heliopolis ('City of the Sun'), now encompassed by modern Cairo. Typically depicted as a falcon with a human body and with a sun disc atop his head, Re could also be shown purely as a sun disc, encircled by a protective cobra, sometimes with outstretched, feathered wings emerging from either side of the disc. Like all Egyptian deities, the sun god manifested himself in a variety of forms. In the morning he was Khepri – the scarab beetle – slowly rolling the great ball of the sun above the horizon; at midday he was Re, the most powerful manifestation of the sun god; and in the evening, he was the weary ram-headed Atum, ready to pass below the horizon into the afterlife realm of the Duat to be re-energized for the coming morning. Another frequently attested manifestation is Re-Horakhety ('Re-Horus of the Two Horizons'), in which Re and Horus were united and associated with the rising and setting sun.

## The Secret Name of the Sun God

As king, Re ruled over both men and gods, and on a daily basis manifested himself in many forms under many names; his own true name, however, was unknown to all but he alone. This was not out of embarrassment, or because he preferred to use a pseudonym, it was for his own security. Knowing a deity's (or even a person's) true name gave an individual power over the deity, allowing him to utilize the god's power for his own purposes. For this reason, gods hid their true names deep in their bellies, to protect them from misuse by magicians.

Isis, a powerful sorceress, 'more rebellious than an infinite number of men, smarter than an infinite number of gods' (see box p. 46) knew this and wanted to become equal in power to Re. If she could learn Re's name and gain his power, she could pass on this knowledge to her unborn (yet to be conceived even) son Horus, ensuring his primary role in the cosmos.

When Re had grown old, Isis implemented her plan. As the sun god sat on his throne, idly drooling on the floor, she collected a small amount of his saliva and kneaded it with some earth to form a snake. Divine fluids are infused with creative power, and her creation sprang to life. At this time, however, the snake remained motionless, and Isis placed it at a crossroads where Re, despite his advanced age, walked each day with his entourage to view creation. Taking his stroll the next day, his eyes weak, the elderly Re failed to spot the snake and was bitten by it. Searing pains burned throughout his body and the fire was so intense that a nearby pine tree burst into flames. Re's screams reached the sky and disturbed the gods. As the poison overwhelmed his body, taking possession of him like the Nile inundation takes possession of the land, the god's lips quivered, his limbs trembled and he was left unable to speak.

Re's pained screams brought his followers to his side. He explained that something had stung him, an unknown creature, one that his eyes did not see, his heart did not know, that his hand did not make, and one that he did not recognize as his creation (surely an extra nagging irritation to the creator of the world). 'I have not tasted a suffering like it; there is no greater pain than this,' Re said, pondering on the creature that attacked him. 'It is not fire, nor is it water – (though) my heart is seized with heat, my body is trembling and my limbs are goose-flesh all over.' The seriousness of his predicament dawning on him, Re asked for the children of the gods to be brought, people conversant with spells and whose words had magic power.

The hawk-headed sun god, Re-Horakhety, sits with the goddess Hathor.

### Isis and the Growth of Her Cult

The goddess Isis was closely associated with magic, motherhood and love. Shown in human form, Isis wears a long dress and sometimes holds a sistrum. The symbol of a throne rests upon her head; this hieroglyph proclaims her name, which itself can be translated as 'seat' or 'throne', highlighting her importance to the kingship. Owing to her close associations with Hathor, Isis is sometimes depicted in a similar manner, with cow horns and a sun disc upon her head. Rarely, she is shown as a rearing cobra, for example in the New Kingdom Book of Gates.

In myth, Isis was the sister–wife of Osiris and one of the four children of Geb and Nut. The myths about the conception of her and Osiris' son Horus, and the child's long struggle for the kingship are told in Chapters 3 and 4. During funerary ceremonies, mourners were associated with Isis and her sister Nephthys, while in the afterlife Isis was believed to sustain the deceased. The Egyptians also associated Isis with the star Sirius, whose annual disappearance and return marked the time of the inundation and the subsequent harvest.

From the Ptolemaic Period, the cult of Isis spread throughout the Mediterranean world, leading her to become assimilated with other notable goddesses, so much so that she became known as 'The One with Many Names'. Her medicinal and curative powers were praised, and she was regarded as a compassionate mother goddess. With the growth of the cult of Isis, Horus became associated with the Greek god Apollo, and came to symbolize the defeat of evil by good.

The children of the gods soon arrived; they crowded around Re, trying to discover a cure, while Isis, standing among them, pretended to know nothing about the creature that had struck down her king. She approached Re, asking him what the problem was: 'A serpent that has brought weakness over you?' she asked. 'One of your children who has raised his head against you?' She promised to slay the evil with her sorcery and cause it to retreat from seeing his rays. Re, covered in sweat, trembling and blind, related again how

Isis wearing the cow horns and sun disc more often associated with Hathor.

he had been stung, complaining, 'Heaven pours rain down into my face in summertime!' The time was right for Isis to play her hand; she told the king that she could only help him if she knew his name. In response, Re, probably battling his delirious state, blurted out a series of his names, many of which described his good deeds for the cosmos: he said that he was the one who made the sky, earth, mountains and water; who made the hours so that days came into existence; and who divided the years. He added that he was Khepri in the morning, Re at noon and Atum in the evening.

The scarab-beetle-headed god Khepri.

Isis was unimpressed, the poison remained in Re's body and the god felt no better. The goddess leaned closer to Re, saying that his true name couldn't have been among those listed. If he wanted to be healed, he'd have to be more forthcoming. The poison bit into Re's body ever stronger, more powerfully than flames. Beaten, he told Isis to listen carefully, so that his true name might leave his belly and enter hers, adding that she could pass it onto her son Horus, so long as he vowed never to tell anybody else. At long last, her plan successful, Isis used her magic to cure the sun god, saying:

*Break out, scorpions! Leave Re! Eye of Horus, leave the god!*
*Flame of the mouth – I am the one who made you, I am*
*the one who sent you – come to the earth, powerful poison!*
*See, the great god has given his name away. Re shall live,*
*once the poison has died!*
PAPYRUS TURIN 1993

It was perhaps such traumatic events that led Re occasionally to punish the gods. One short myth refers to Re summoning all the gods and goddesses and, upon their arrival, swallowing them. While they wriggled inside his body, he killed them and vomited them up as birds and fish. Nevertheless, there wasn't always a scheming god behind Re's illnesses. In one myth, Re falls ill and can only be cured by the powerful denizens of the Duat. To reach these after-life dwellers, the god's entourage write a letter to the authorities of Heliopolis, worried that Re may become stuck in the Duat if his pains continue, and ask that an appeal be made to the people of the West (the dead), by shouting through a hole in the ground. Another myth presents Re as collapsing after treading on an un-named crea-ture, and feeling convulsions. On this occasion, the unlucky god had to reveal the true name of his mother in order to be cured.

### The Myth of the Eye of the Sun

During Re's reign, he and his Eye quarrelled so much that the Eye decided to leave, storming off to Libya or Nubia, depending on the variant of the myth, and attacking everyone she met along the way. Her absence, however, left Re defenceless from his enemies, as she served as his protection and was crucial to his own power. To rectify the situation, Re sent out a god to retrieve the angry Eye. As ever, there are many variants of this myth, and the names of the gods involved change accordingly: one version tells that Onuris

Onuris (left), wearing double plumes on his head, and his wife, the lion-headed goddess Mekhit.

### Onuris (Anhur)

Onuris was a god of war and hunting, whose origins lie in the area of Abydos. He is typically depicted as a bearded man, standing upright and with a short wig surmounted by a uraeus and two to four plumes. He raises his right hand, and often holds a length of rope in his left. His name means, 'he who leads back the distant one', a reference to his mythical role as the god who brought back the leonine Eye of Re from Nubia; she then became his wife, Mekhit. This myth is virtually identical to that of Shu bringing back the Eye of Re as Tefnut, which was probably derived from the Onuris myth. Consequently, Onuris was often equated with Shu, the more dominant god in the pantheon, and was regarded as a son of Re, who hunted and slew the enemies of the sun god.

(see box above) tracked down the Eye and married her afterwards. Another version presents Shu hunting for her. In the longest preserved account, however, it is Thoth, a god famous for his counsel and wisdom (see box opposite), who travels to seek out the Eye. In this variant, the Eye is named as Tefnut and takes the form of a Nubian cat.

After tracking down the Eye, and in order to approach her without being recognized, Thoth transformed himself into a dog-faced baboon, but Tefnut saw through his ruse and became enraged, ready to attack the god. Thoth, thinking quickly, told her that fate punishes every crime. His wise words convinced her to halt her

### Thoth and the *Corpus Hermeticum*

The god Thoth, depicted as an ibis, an ibis-headed man, or as a squatting baboon, was a moon god associated with wisdom, knowledge and learning; given Thoth's lunar associations, it is possible that the ibis' long curved beak was thought to resemble the crescent moon. In his baboon form, he often wears a full and crescent moon combined upon his head.

The Egyptians regarded Thoth as the inventor of writing, and as a protector of scribes. He was a master of magic and secret knowledge, who recorded the passage of time and oversaw the weighing of the deceased's heart in the afterlife; his presence was an assurance that all affairs would be conducted fairly. Though normally presented as a diplomat, whose wise words counselled the gods, in the Pyramid Texts Thoth performs violent acts against the enemies of *maat*.

Thoth is sometimes presented as the result of the union between Horus and Seth, however, other inscriptions describe him as a son of Re or Horus. His wife was Nehemetawy, while the goddess of writing, Seshat, was his daughter (though sometimes she replaces Nehemetawy as his wife). Thoth's main cult centre was at Hermopolis (modern El-Ashmunein) in Middle Egypt; to the priests of Hermopolis, Thoth appeared on the first mound of creation and created the Ogdoad, the first gods in existence.

As Thoth was also a divine messenger, the Greeks associated him with their god Hermes, calling him the 'Thrice Great Hermes' or Hermes Trismegistus. In this form, he was believed to have passed on his teachings to disciples, his wise words collated as the *Corpus Hermeticum* in the first centuries AD. Thanks to Byzantine editors and copyists, these important teachings were preserved, enabling them to influence Renaissance thinkers over a thousand years later, especially regarding their approach to magic and alchemy.

unprovoked attack. Having gained Tefnut's attention, and in the hope of convincing her to return home, Thoth extolled the beauty of Egypt and regaled her with a series of animal fables (sometimes placing a fable within a fable), infused with moral lessons on the importance of peace and how the strong benefit from friendship with the weak. In the process, Tefnut, angered by Thoth's attempts to influence her, transformed into a terrifying lioness, but Thoth refused to give up. He succeeded in convincing her to return to Egypt, and they were met at the border with music and dancing. When they had arrived in Memphis, Re organized a festival in Tefnut's honour at the Mansion of the Lady of the Sycamore – a chapel of Hathor (see box p. 58) – and she recounted to Re the tales that Thoth had told her. The sun god then praised Thoth for his success.

## Some Myths of Rebellion against the Sun God

A frequent theme of myths set during the reign of Re are rebellions against his rule. The locations of the rebellions vary, as do the identities of those involved: sometimes it is humanity, at other times it is Apophis and his followers, or even Seth (see box p. 55). Another variant is the age of the sun god – sometimes he is a child, while in some myths he is elderly. In both cases, the creator is at a vulnerable stage in life, which explains why the rebellions erupt at this time. These two phases of the sun god's life represent sunrise and sunset – traditional periods of danger – or signify his weakening over the course of the solar year, until his rebirth and renewal at the new year.

### The Rebellion in the Neith Cosmogony from Esna

At the Temple of Esna, a myth recounts a rebellion that occurred during the sun god's youth. After his creation from Neith's discarded spittle (see p. 38), Apophis immediately conceived rebellion in his heart, and his plans for revolt were aided by his associates among mankind. Re, learning of Apophis' plans, became bitter, and Thoth emerged from the sun god's heart to debate the situation with him. Re decided to send Thoth, as 'Lord of the Words of the God', to battle Apophis, while he himself fled to safety with his mother, who had by this time manifested in the form of the celestial Ihet-cow, who became known as Mehet-Weret 'the great swimmer'. Re sat on her brow between her horns while she swam to Sais in the north, where they could hide in safety. There, Re's mother breastfed the young god, making him strong enough to return south to massacre his enemies.

### The Book of the Faiyum

This composition, first found during the Ptolemaic Period, includes a number of myths from Egypt's Faiyum Oasis; among them is a tale of rebellion against Re. The sun god heard that men and gods were plotting against him, and went to fight them at Herakleopolis, an important city, just south of the Faiyum. He was victorious, but before a second battle could commence, the aged god withdrew to the town of Moeris in the Faiyum in order to seek refuge with his mother, the Ihet-cow (here a personification of Lake Moeris). Safe, the god hid for 12 months, suckling his mother's rejuvenating milk, before the two flew to the heavens, Re upon his mother's back, where she transformed into the sky.

### A Myth of Rebellion from Kom Ombo

This myth from Kom Ombo in Upper Egypt, the location of a temple dedicated to Sobek and Horus the Elder, also begins with Re's enemies plotting against him. Learning of their plans, Re, along with Thoth and Horus the Elder (see box p. 56), went in search of them, tracking their movements to Kom Ombo. Arriving at the city, Re settled in his palace and sent Thoth to seek out and spy on his enemies. The wise god found them camped on the shore of a great lake, and, from a safe distance, standing on the banks of a river, counted 257 enemies, led by eight officers. All were standing around, slandering the sun god. Thoth swiftly returned to Re to report all that he had seen.

Naturally, Re became enraged and announced that he would not allow a single one of them to live. Perhaps a little too tired to engage in battle himself, or just wary of the enemies' numbers, Thoth suggested Horus the Elder (in this myth an aspect of the god Shu) as a suitably skilled warrior to annihilate Re's enemies. Re followed his advice and sent out Horus the Elder armed with all his weapons of war; he slaughtered with such rage and violence that his face turned crimson from the blood.

### The Legend of the Winged Sun Disc at Edfu

A particularly detailed myth of rebellion against the sun god is preserved in Ptolemaic Period inscription on the walls of the Temple of Horus at Edfu. In the 363rd year of Re's reign, the sun god and his entourage were sailing in Nubia when Horus of Behdet (the ancient name of Edfu) spotted enemies – associates of the trickster god Seth – plotting against the king. In a pre-emptive strike, Re sent out against them Horus, who flew up into the sky as a great winged disc. 'He stormed against them before him', we are told, 'and they neither saw with their eyes nor heard with their ears, but [each] one slew his fellow in the twinkling of an eye, and not a soul lived.' Faced with the bloodthirsty god, the enemies had lost their senses and begun to swing their weapons around, slashing one another instead of their opponent. Re then descended from his solar boat to view his fallen enemies, who lay on the ground 'with broken heads'.

As the crew of the solar boat celebrated, more enemies arrived and launched an attack, taking the fearsome forms of crocodiles and hippopotami. In retaliation, Horus and his followers fought them with harpoons. The enemies that survived this divine onslaught fled north, but Horus took chase and slaughtered most of them near Thebes. The remaining survivors continued north, but Horus followed, sailing in the barque of Re.

Seth roared with anger at the slaughter Horus had led, and the two began to fight. Horus threw his spear at Seth, and hurled him

## Seth

A god associated with violence, confusion and evil, Seth can be depicted as a creature with a long snout, tall rectangular ears and an erect tail; in human form, he only bears the creature's head. He can, however, manifest in many other forms too, including that of a red ox, a desert oryx, a pig or a hippopotamus.

According to Pyramid Text 205, Seth tore himself from his mother Nut during birth, highlighting his violent nature from the start of his life. He was the brother of Osiris, whom he murdered to become king of Egypt, and later became embroiled in a lengthy legal battle with his nephew Horus for the throne (see below). Various goddesses are cited as Seth's consort; most frequently, Nephthys is said to be his wife, though Taweret, Neith, Astarte and Anat are also mentioned.

As lord of the Red Land, Seth was god of the desert, yet he was also connected with storms (his voice was thunder), cloudy weather and the sea, and could be prayed to for calmer weather. He also presided over foreign countries. Though he is often presented as an enemy, Seth used his great strength to protect the sun god Re from the chaos snake Apophis during his nightly journey through the Duat. Unlike most gods, whose bones were said to be of silver, Seth's were formed from iron, and he could be described as lord of metals. Many temples were dedicated to Seth, especially in the northeast Delta, but his primary cult centre was at Nubt (Ombos) at the entrance to the Wadi Hammamat, a source of gold.

---

to the ground, taking the god prisoner by binding his hands and tying a rope around his throat. Defeated and embarrassed, Seth was brought before Re and his entourage for his fate to be decided.

Thoth, as advisor to the sun god, suggested that Seth's followers be given to Isis, so that she could do whatever she wished with them. Not the most forgiving of deities, Horus and Isis beheaded them all, leaving Seth, no doubt aware that he was next on the hit list, to transform into a snake and disappear into the ground. Afterwards,

### Which Horus? Horus of Behdet, Horus the Falcon, Horus the Elder and Horus the Child

There is a confusing array of Horus figures in Egyptian mythology and though often treated as separate gods with different parents, they should each be regarded as aspects of the same divinity.

Horus of Behdet, from the *Legend of the Winged Sun Disc*, is the form of the god worshipped at the Temple of Edfu in Upper Egypt and possibly at Tell el-Balamun in the Delta. He was the husband of Hathor and father of the gods Horus Uniter-of-the-Two-Lands (Horus-Sematawy or Harsomtus) and Ihy. Like all forms of Horus, he is typically shown as a hawk, often hovering over the pharaoh, though he could also be depicted as a lion. The winged sun disc, carved into temple walls across Egypt, and most often seen decorating lintels, is also an image of Horus of Behdet.

The god Horus as a falcon wearing the Double Crown of Upper and Lower Egypt.

Horus the Falcon, whose cult centre was at Hierakonpolis (Nekhen) in the south of Egypt, was a god of kingship, associated with Egypt's kings from the earliest periods. As a sky god, Horus the Falcon's eyes were regarded as the sun and moon.

Horus the Elder, depicted as a man with a falcon's head, was the son of Nut and Geb, or Hathor and Re, depending on the variant of the myth. He fathered the Four Sons of Horus (see box p. 174) with his (sometime) sister, Isis. The early Pyramid Texts present Horus the Elder as helping Isis and Nephthys to gather together the pieces of Osiris' body, and then avenge him.

Horus the Child, typically shown as a child with a sidelock of youth, was the son of Isis and Osiris. He was added to the Pyramid Texts in the 6th Dynasty, and absorbed into the Heliopolitan mythology.

Horus continued to chase the remaining enemies all the way to the Mediterranean Sea, before turning his attention southward, finding and killing a final group of enemies in Nubia.

## Beer Saves the World

When Re reached old age, his bones silver, his flesh gold and his hair lapis lazuli, mankind (as usual) plotted against him. Before they could launch their assault, however, Re discovered their nefarious plans and commanded that his Eye be summoned, along with Shu, Tefnut, Geb, Nut, the fathers and mothers who were with Re when he was in Nun (meaning the eight primordial gods), Nun himself and Nun's courtiers. The sun god wished to consult them for advice, but wanted to ensure that mankind wouldn't suspect a thing, so they were brought to his palace in secret.

The gods and courtiers duly assembled in two rows before the sun god, who was sitting upon his throne. 'O eldest god in whom I came into being [Nun], and ancestor gods,' Re said. 'Look, mankind, which issued from my Eye, is plotting against me. Tell me what you would do about it, for I am searching. I would not slay them until I have heard what you might say about it.' Having considered the options, Nun advised Re that fear of him was greatest when his Eye was upon those who schemed against him. Re knew that the rebels had fled to the desert, 'their hearts fearful that I might speak to them', and decided to follow Nun's suggestion – he sent out his Eye to smite them.

The Eye took the wrathful form of Hathor, and immediately began to slaughter with utmost relish, first killing the enemies in the desert, and then turning on everyone else. Witnessing the indiscriminate destruction of his creation, Re had second thoughts and convinced himself that with some extra effort, he could continue to rule over mankind as king. The only problem now was Hathor – his Eye – who was rather enjoying massacring everyone she met. If Re were to stop her, he'd have to devise a cunning plan.

---

**Hathor**

Meaning 'House of Horus', in human form, Hathor can be identified by her long black wig, tied with a filet, surmounted by a uraeus and sun disc, set between two cows' horns. Sometimes she can be seen wearing a vulture headdress. Hathor is also commonly depicted as a divine cow, again wearing a sun disc between her horns. In a third form, she appears human, staring full-faced at the viewer, but displays cow's ears and wears a wig.

At Dendera, Hathor was presented as the wife of Horus, with whom she bore her sons Ihy and Horus-Sematawy (Horus Uniter-of-the-Two-Lands). Other sources present her as wife of the sun god Re, though she can also be named his mother and, in her manifestation as his Eye, his daughter.

As a divine cow, Hathor protected the king and acted as his royal nurse, just as she had nursed the child Horus in Khemmis; she is also said to be the king's wife and mother. To the general population of Egypt, however, she was associated with love, female sexuality, fertility and motherhood, providing divine assistance with all aspects of childbirth. They also identified her with joy, music, dance and alcoholic drinks. As the Mistress of the Sycamore, representing the natural world's fertility, she gave shade, air, food and drink to the dead, while as Mistress of the West, she looked after those buried at Thebes, welcoming them into the afterlife. Hathor was also associated with minerals and resources brought from the deserts and foreign lands, especially turquoise and copper, and protected those working in remote mining areas.

Though many cult centres were associated with Hathor, her most prominent temple, at least in later Egyptian history, was at Dendera.

---

To bring an end to the violence, Re sent messengers to Elephantine, far in the south of Egypt, with orders to bring back red ochre. After receiving the raw mineral, he told the High Priest of Re at Heliopolis to grind it up until it resembled human blood. He then mixed it with seven thousand jars of beer. During the night,

The goddess Sekhmet.

Re sent the beer to where Hathor – now in the overtly violent form of Sekhmet – was resting, and had it poured into the fields, in the hope that when the goddess awoke she would believe herself to be surrounded by blood, her new favourite drink. Just as planned, Hathor-Sekhmet opened her eyes the next morning to a sanguine dream; she drank until drunk, and quickly forgot all about her anger towards mankind.

### Re's Departure
Despite saving mankind, Re decided that he was too weary to continue ruling Egypt personally. The gods tried to dissuade him from leaving, but he was adamant – it was time to go. 'My body is weak for

the first time,' he told them. 'I won't wait until another [rebellion] gets to me.' Reluctantly accepting Re's decision, Nun told Shu that his eye would serve as Re's protection and that Nut should allow the sun god to sit on her back. This confused the sky goddess, who was unprepared for such an unexpected responsibility and unsure of the logistics involved. 'How exactly will Re sit on my back?' she asked Nun. 'Don't be silly,' he responded, as Nut transformed into a cow, providing ample back space for the elderly sun god. As Re took his place atop the newly bovine Nut, men approached, explaining that they had come to overthrow his enemies and anyone who plotted against him. Re ignored them, however, and departed for his palace, leaving Egypt to fall into darkness.

At dawn the next day, Re awoke to discover that mankind had developed bows and clubs to shoot at their enemies. Angered, the sun god announced, 'Your baseness be behind you, O slaughterers; may your slaughtering be far removed [from me].' Their actions strengthened Re's decision to leave; he commanded Nut to raise him into the sky, saying, 'Stay far away from them!' They rose into the sky, and Nut remained with Re through both the day and night, helping him to make some final adjustments to the cosmos: from his distant position in the sky, Re commanded Nut to create the Milky Way. He himself then formed the Field of Reeds and Field of Offerings, both locations associated with the dead, as well as the planets and the stars. When Nut began to tremble because of the great height, Re created the Infinite Ones, two groups of four gods, charged with assisting Shu to support her.

Re then summoned Geb to provide him with instruction: 'Take heed because of your snakes which are in you!' he commanded, in reference to the snakes that hide in the earth (Geb's body). 'See, they feared me when I was there. Also you have become acquainted with their magical power. Go now to the place where my father Nun is and tell him to keep watch over terrestrial and aquatic snakes.' He added that Geb should draw up notices to be placed on the mounds

A scene from the Book of the Heavenly Cow. The cow
is supported by the god Shu and the eight *heh*-gods.

where snakes dwell, telling them to 'beware of disturbing anything'.
'They should know that I am here', Re proclaimed, 'for I am shining
for them.' For all time, Geb was to keep an eye on the snakes' magic
and watch over them.

Having spoken to Geb, Re summoned Thoth and installed him
as the moon and as vizier (his divine deputy, an office paralleled in
the bureaucracy of the pharaoh's court). Re also embraced Nun and
told the gods who ascend in the eastern sky to give praise to Nun as
eldest god in whom he (Re) himself originated. Re then made his
final statement to creation:

> *It is I who made the sky and set [it] in place in order to install
> the* bau *of the gods in it so that I am with them for the eternal
> recurrence [of time] produced through the years. My* ba *is Magic.
> It is [even] greater than this.*

THE BOOK OF THE HEAVENLY COW

A god's *ba* or *bau* (in the plural, for gods could have many *ba*)
was a form through which he or she could be felt or experienced on

earth, a manifestation of divine force and personality. In this newly re-organized world, wind was the *ba* of Shu, for example, the rain the *ba* of Heh; night was the *ba* of darkness, and Re himself the *ba* of Nun; crocodiles were the *bau* of the god Sobek, while the *ba* of Osiris was the sacred ram of Mendes. The *ba* of each deity dwelled within snakes. The *ba* of Apophis was in the Eastern Mountain and the *ba* of Re was in magic throughout the world.

## Re's Retribution for the Rebellions

Re not only punished mankind by distancing himself from the earth, he also shortened human life-spans:

> *They have made war, they have stirred up turmoil, they*
> *have made evil, they have created rebellion, they have done*
> *slaughter, they have created imprisonment. Moreover, they have*
> *made [what was] great into [what is] little in all that I have*
> *made. Show greatness, Thoth, says he, [namely] [Re]-Atum.*
> *You shall not see [further] wrongdoing, you shall not endure [it].*
> *Shorten their years, cut short their months since they have done*
> *hidden damage to all that you have made.*
> BOOK OF THE DEAD, SPELL 175

#### ◄ THE REIGN OF KING SHU ►

Re withdrew to the heavens and his son, Shu, took his place as king, ruling as the perfect god of heaven, land, Duat, water and wind. He swiftly smote those that had rebelled against his father and sacrificed the children of Apophis. Afterwards, as the air cooled and the ground became dry, Shu erected cities and founded nomes (the administrative regions of the Nile Valley and Delta), defended the borders of Egypt and built temples in the north and south. All was well, except for his relationship with his troublesome son, Geb. At one time, Geb transformed into a boar and swallowed the Eye of Re that remained with Shu to protect him. Though Geb denied this act, the Eye bled from his skin like a disease, and had to be put back in place on the horizon by Thoth. Geb then attacked Shu, and was forced to drink urine as punishment. Geb also enraged his father by taking the form of a bull and having sexual intercourse with his own mother, Tefnut; as before, at first he refused to admit his crime to Shu, but a lance thrust into his thigh loosened his tongue.

One day, while residing in Memphis, Shu summoned the Great Ennead of gods and told them that they were to accompany him on a walk eastward, to a place where he could meet his father, Re-Horakhety (Re in his form as Horus of the Horizon), and spend some time with him. They happily obliged, and soon afterwards the royal court had taken up residence at the abdicated king's earthly home. It was not to be a pleasant experience, however. While the gods enjoyed the company of Re, the children of Apophis, marauding rebels of the desert, arrived from the east, intent on causing havoc. Their aim was not to conquer territory, but to destroy; any territory that they passed through, whether on land or water, lay abandoned, scorched and uninhabitable in their wake. Hearing of the chaos afflicting Egypt's east, Shu mustered his followers and the followers of Re, and ordered his men to take up positions on the hills of Iat-Nebes (modern Saft el-Henna, a site in the desert just southeast of the Delta). These hills had existed since the time of King Re, and would serve as a perfect defensive line from which to protect the sun god and Egypt. As expected, the Children of Apophis arrived and battle began; Shu quickly slaughtered his enemies and drove back all who opposed his father.

Shu may have won the battle, but he did not win the war. Shortly after his success over the children of Apophis, revolution erupted in Shu's palace, led by a band of rebels. Overwhelmed, the land fell into chaos and Shu, like his father, ascended into the sky, leaving his wife Tefnut behind on earth. Perhaps fleeing the surrounding

Thoth (right) inscribes the length of the king's reign on the sacred *ished* (persea) tree.

danger, Tefnut left Memphis at midday to visit another, more secure palace elsewhere, but instead found her way to Pekharety, a town in Syria-Palestine. As during the reign of Re, when Tefnut, in her form as the sun god's Eye, attempted to leave Egypt, but was brought back by Onuris, Shu or Thoth, on this occasion Geb went in search of his mother and returned her to the palace.

Not that Egypt was any safer than foreign lands. A great turmoil still engulfed the palace, and a powerful storm arose, one so intense that neither human nor god could see one another. Nobody left the palace for nine days, not until the chaos abated and the weather returned to normal. Now, finally, Geb formally ascended the throne of his father, and his courtiers kissed the ground in his presence. Geb then honoured his father's name on the sacred mythical *ished*-tree of Heliopolis, which bore the name of each king of Egypt, inscribed by Thoth, along with the length of their reigns.

### ◀ THE REIGN OF KING GEB ▶

A short time after ascending the throne, Geb left his palace to travel to the Egyptian Delta, following his father as he flew through the sky, to visit the town of Iat-Nebes. Upon arrival, Geb enquired about the locality, asking the gods to tell him of everything that had happened there to Re, of any battles that had occurred, as well as of any events concerning Shu. As they regaled Geb with the tale of Shu's great victory against the children of Apophis, they mentioned that the former ruler had worn a living uraeus – a rearing cobra – on his head. This was news to Geb, who now desired to wear the living uraeus himself, just as his father had done. Unfortunately, it had been sealed in a chest, hidden somewhere in Pi-Yaret (near modern Saft el-Henna in the Delta), and would first need to be located. Such trivialities would not deter the newly crowned king, however: without delay, he assembled his followers, and set out on his quest for the living uraeus.

Geb and his entourage quickly discovered the chest's location, but as the divine king leaned forward to open the lid, the uraeus leapt from within and breathed a great flame against him. Geb's followers died instantly, incinerated by the force of the fire. The king survived, but with his head badly burnt. Reeling from the pain, Geb made his way to the Field of the Henu-Plants to search for relief, but found none. He then commanded one of his followers to bring the Wig of Re, a magical item, infused with power, regarded as the only object capable of healing his wounds. The wig successfully healed Geb, and later performed further miracles; for one, it transformed into a crocodile, who became known as Sobek of Iat-Nebes.

Healed and resting in his residence at Itj-Tawy, just north of the Faiyum Oasis, Geb's next act was to despatch a military force against rebellious Asiatics, bringing large numbers back to Egypt as prisoners. He then listened to more tales of the reign of Shu, before asking for a list of all places that both Re and Shu had commanded be built on earth. Most of these locations had been destroyed by the rebellious children of Apophis, so Geb commanded that they be rebuilt. Millions of settlements were re-founded and their names were recorded in great lists (including on the side of the naos from which this myth derives), testaments to Geb's good deeds for Egypt.

Despite his successes as ruler, Geb saw in his son, Osiris, a worthy king of Egypt, a god who could lead the land to good fortune, and so decided to abdicate his throne, just as Shu and Re had done before him. He awarded Osiris the land, 'its water, its wind, its plants, and all its cattle. All that flies, all that alights, its reptiles and its desert game…' Thus, Osiris became king, and a new era in the reign of the gods began.

# ◄ 3 ►

## THE REIGN OF KING OSIRIS

With the abdication of Geb, the crown passed to his son Osiris, a god associated with fertility and regeneration, who in death – for Egyptian gods were not immune to death – became king of the Duat and ruler of the blessed dead. In art, Osiris is depicted as a tightly wrapped mummy, standing upright or sitting enthroned, with skin coloured green or black to represent the fertile soil. He holds the crook and flail of a pharaoh in his hands, and wears an elaborate collar around his neck, as well as the *atef*-crown on his head. This crown is similar to the pharaonic White Crown of Upper Egypt, being tall and tapering to a bulbous peak, but with the addition of two tall plumes at the sides; it is sometimes embellished with sun discs and horns.

#### ◄ CORONATION AND RULE ►

Re crowned Osiris with the *atef*-crown in the Heliopolitan Nome, but the crown's powerful heat was such that it caused the new king to fall ill; its effects were so long lasting that after the ceremony, Re found Osiris sitting in his house, his face all swollen. It was an inauspicious start to his reign, but Osiris quickly gained the reputation of being a great and benevolent king; indeed, he was well prepared for the job, having served as vizier, chief priest of Heliopolis and royal herald before inheriting the crown. And, standing 8 cubits, 6 palms and 3 fingers tall (about 4.7m or 15.4ft), he could certainly intimidate any enemies on the battlefield. His reign is described as a time of prosperity, when all resources were well controlled and the land was stable. Life was good, the disordered waters of Nun were kept at

Osiris wears the *atef*-crown, with the crook and flail of kingship in his hands.

bay, the cold north wind blew (something particularly longed for in the fierce Egyptian heat) and animals procreated. Conspirators were crushed and Osiris was respected among the gods. In fact, the only significant problem faced by Osiris during his early reign happened when, one night, a storm hit Egypt and the goddess Sekhmet had to save him using her power over water.

In later legend, preserved for posterity by two Greek historians, Diodorus Siculus and Plutarch (who wrote in the 1st century BC and the 2nd century AD respectively), we find that the establishment of various social structures and customs was attributed to Osiris during his reign. Plutarch relates how, as king, the god taught the Egyptians how to cultivate the land; he also gave them laws and taught them to honour the gods. According to Diodorus Siculus, Osiris did many good deeds for the social life of mankind, for a start, making them give up cannibalism – since Isis had discovered wheat and barley, they took up eating these instead of each other. Isis also established laws, while Osiris built temples to his parents and other gods at Thebes. Both deities honoured those who nurtured the arts and made technological advances. One advance in particular was the development of copper tools, which helped people to kill animals and conduct agricultural activities more effectively. According to Diodorus, Osiris was the first to invent and taste wine, and he took counsel with Thoth on every matter. Another source describes Khentiamentu, a deity who is normally a form of Osiris, serving as the god-king's vizier. The god Hu (the personification of authority) served as Osiris' general in Upper Egypt, while Sia (perception) was his general in Lower Egypt.

The ibis-headed god Thoth.

Afterwards, both Diodorus and Plutarch relate, Osiris gathered a great army and travelled the world teaching its population about wine and how to sow wheat and barley, leaving Isis (his sister–wife, with whom he had apparently begun his relationship in the womb) to rule Egypt in his absence with Thoth as her counsel. Osiris took his sons Anubis (see box p. 174) and Macedon (a Greek name, substituting for the Egyptian god Wepwawet) along with him, as well as Pan (Min). His army consisted of men experienced in agriculture, musicians, singers and dancers – Osiris was apparently fond of laughter, food and entertainment. Plutarch says that he would win over those he met through charm and persuasiveness, along with the allure of music and dance.

Like many gap-year students, when he set off on his travels Osiris decided to let his hair grow until returning home. First, he marched south into Ethiopia, where he founded cities, taught people the wonders of agriculture and left men to rule in his name; these were

Osiris, tightly wrapped like a mummy, and Isis stand before the four sons of Horus.

trusted individuals from whom he could collect tribute. Eventually, he made his way to India and founded further cities. Osiris' journey was not entirely peaceful, however; in Thrace, for example, he slew the king of the barbarians. After making his way around the entire world, Osiris returned to Egypt with countless exotic gifts.

◄ THE CHILDREN OF OSIRIS ►

According to Plutarch, Osiris had an affair with his sister Nephthys, wife of Seth, believing her to be Isis (well, they do look alike). Despite the shock of this infidelity, Isis went in search of the child born of her husband's adulterous union because Nephthys had left him exposed – a typically Roman practice, and so perhaps a detail added to the myth by Plutarch – out of fear of Seth's retribution for her extramarital affair. After much trouble, Isis tracked down the child with the help of dogs. She brought the child up and he became her guardian, Anubis.

Anubis was not Osiris' first child, however. Although his most famous child, by his sister–wife Isis, is Horus the Child (see box p. 56), he first fathered an obscure daughter, known only from a spell of late Middle Kingdom date, who had the role of moulding mud-bricks. Apparently, she had been of the opinion that Osiris should live only on *djais*-plants (a form of poisonous herb) and honey, which is bitter to those of the Duat – Osiris' afterlife home. Given these sentiments, she was perhaps sent to mould mud-bricks as a form of punishment for her murderous thoughts towards her father. The god Babi, an aggressive divine baboon, who lived on human entrails (see box p. 188), was also said to be the eldest son of Osiris, and Sopdet, the personification of the brightest star in the sky, Sirius, to be another daughter. In the Coffin Texts, the jackal god Wepwawet, associated with funerals and cemeteries, is also described as a son of Osiris.

---

**Nephthys**

Typically depicted in human form as a goddess, but sometimes as a kite, Nephthys (meaning 'Mistress of the Mansion') was one of the four children of Nut and Geb, and wife to her brother Seth. According to later legend, she was also the mother of Anubis. In myth, she helped her sister, Isis, to protect and resurrect Osiris, mourned his death with her and helped guard Horus from Seth. She played a similarly protective role for the deceased; her image is often found on sarcophagi, and she, along with the god Hapy, guarded the lungs of the dead, kept separately from the mummified body in a canopic jar. Nephthys had no cult centre of her own, but is found frequently on amulets from the 26th Dynasty onwards.

---

◄ THE MURDER OF OSIRIS BY SETH ►

The only complete reconstructions of the story of Osiris' death come from accounts provided by the Greek authors we met above, Diodorus Siculus and Plutarch. Ancient Egyptian sources shine little light on what happened because to describe the god's death in any detail was against decorum. Here we shall first recreate the full account from the Greek sources and then show how they are backed up by details from ancient Egyptian texts from tombs and papyri. Although Plutarch's account is later in date, it is the fuller of the two and we begin with it.

**The Osiris Myth According to Plutarch and Diodorus**

After Osiris returned home from his travels, his brother Seth plotted against him, gathering 72 conspirators and working in co-operation with an Ethiopian queen. Seth secretly measured Osiris' body and made a beautiful chest to his size, ornamented with jewels. He ordered it be brought into a chamber where festivities were being held, so that everyone present could marvel at its beauty. His guests suitably impressed, Seth announced that whoever best fitted the chest when lying within could keep it. Enticed by his offer, the guests took turns trying to fit inside, but without success, until Osiris lay within and found it perfectly matched his size. At that moment, Seth's conspirators leapt forward and sealed it shut, hammering nails into its wooden frame and pouring molten lead over any gaps. Without wasting time, they hurled the chest into the river and watched as it sailed along the Nile towards the sea. This is said to have occurred in either the 28th year of Osiris' reign or of his life.

Hearing of these macabre events, Isis, in the city of Koptos, cut off a tress of hair and donned a garment of mourning. She wandered at her wits end, until one day she came across a group of children and asked if they had seen the chest. Luckily for her, they had, though at the time it was heading towards the sea. After further investigation, Isis learnt that the chest had made its way to Byblos, where the sea had deposited it in a clump of heather. There it had grown into a great tree, which concealed the chest within its trunk. Unwilling to waste any further time, Isis set off to retrieve the chest, but while she travelled, the king of Byblos came to the seashore to admire the great size of the tree. Wanting a sturdy pillar to support the roof of his palace, he cut down the thickest section of the tree – the part concealing Osiris' chest – and took it home with him, so that, when Isis arrived, she found nothing but the remains of the trunk. She sat by a spring, dejected and tearful, and there met the queen's maidservants. She spoke with them, plaited their hair and gave them a wondrous fragrance. When the maidservants returned to the palace, the queen smelt their perfume and immediately asked for Isis to be brought before her; she then appointed Isis as nurse to her baby.

Each night, while the king and queen slept, Isis magically burnt away the mortal portions of the baby prince's body, and transformed into a swallow to fly around the pillar that bore the corpse of Osiris, wailing and lamenting the loss of her husband. One night,

Mourned by Isis (right) and Nephthys (left), the god Osiris lies on his funerary bier.

the queen heard the noise outside her bedroom door and crept out to investigate. Finding her baby on fire, she screamed, halting Isis' magic and denying the baby prince immortality. Discovered, Isis now displayed her true form as a goddess and demanded the pillar. The queen, unable to deny the request, looked on as Isis removed the pillar (luckily it wasn't load bearing) and cut away at the wood until the chest was revealed. Isis immediately threw herself upon the coffin wailing; so intense were the goddesses emotions, that the baby prince dropped dead.

Returning to Egypt, Isis hid the chest, but Seth, out hunting one night by the light of the moon, came across it. Recognizing the body, he tore it into 14 pieces and scattered them across Egypt. Isis learned of his desecration and sailed through the swamps in a papyrus boat, searching for the pieces of her husband. She found every part of Osiris' body, except for his phallus, which had been eaten by Nile fish, so she fashioned a replacement instead. Plutarch relates here that some myths present Isis holding a separate funeral for each body part wherever she found it, explaining why so many locations claim Osiris' tomb. Other myths report that she only pretended to bury parts of the body in these locations so as to receive more divine honours for her husband. Multiple burials also had the added benefit of preventing Seth from ever discovering the god's true tomb.

Diodorus' (earlier) account of Osiris' death is a little more succinct. He relates how Seth murdered his brother and cut the body into 26 pieces, each of which was given to one of his followers. But Isis and Horus (presumably the Elder Horus, see box p. 56, who does not feature in Plutarch's account) took revenge, slaughtering Seth and his followers. Afterwards, Isis sought out and gathered together all the pieces of Osiris, except for his penis, which had been lost. To protect her husband's body from Seth (seemingly immune to slaughter), Isis decided to keep his burial place a secret, but this created a dilemma: how could the people of Egypt honour Osiris if there was no tomb to visit?

Her solution was ingenious: she took each part of Osiris' body, and formed a complete replica of his shape from spices and wax, so that irrespective of the body part presented, Osiris appeared complete. She then summoned priests in separate groups, and bestowed upon each of them their own 'corpse', explaining that this was the true body of Osiris and instructing them to look after it by burying it in their district and performing daily cult offerings. Honoured, each group of priests departed to build a tomb for the dead god. For this reason, very many locations across Egypt claimed the true burial of Osiris. Diodorus adds that Isis vowed never to remarry and spent her life ruling Egypt. She became immortal in death and was buried near Memphis.

## Ancient Egyptian Sources for the Osiris Myth

The paucity of Egyptian sources for the myth of Osiris' death is complicated also by the fact that the myth changed over the thousands of years of Egyptian history, with the first evidence for it found in the Pyramid Texts (see box p. 129) inscribed on the walls of the pyramid of King Unas of the Old Kingdom.

### The Account in the Pyramid Texts

From scattered references across the Pyramid Text spells, it is possible to reconstruct that Isis and Nephthys, in the form of kites, went in search of the body of Osiris, who had been 'thrown to the ground' on the river banks at Nedyt by Seth (seemingly because Osiris had kicked him). Upon finding the body, Isis and Nephthys made the ritual gestures of mourning: Isis sat with her arms atop her head, and Nephthys seized the tips of her breasts. The goddesses managed to halt Osiris' decay by preventing his bodily fluids from dripping to the ground and by stopping his corpse from smelling foul. Finally, through ritual and magic, they revived their brother.

A variant of the myth in the Pyramid Texts tells that Osiris' body was discovered in Geheset, 'Gazelle-land', after he had been 'felled on his side' by Seth. Further spells, however, indicate that Osiris drowned, or at least that he was thrown into the water after he had been killed. This detail, that Osiris died by drowning, is in fact supported by later texts: an inscription, probably from the New Kingdom, quotes Horus' command to Isis and Nephthys that they grasp Osiris to save him from becoming submerged in the water that had drowned him. An early 26th Dynasty papyrus also refers to Osiris as having been thrown into the river and floating all the way to Imet in the northeast Delta.

### Papyrus Salt 825

Papyrus Salt 825, whose text is a 'Ritual for the End of Mummification Operations' that incorporates elements of this myth, places Osiris in Tawer, 'the Great Land' – a reference to the nome in which Abydos, his main cult centre, was traditionally found – at the time of his death. Seth intercepted Osiris there, attacking him within Nedyt

The goddess Isis as a kite.

in Hatdjefau (two locations in Abydos). Under the *aru*-tree, on the 17th day of the first month of inundation, Seth committed an act of violence against Osiris and threw him into the waters. The god Nun, as water, rose to cover Osiris' body and took him away to hide his mysteries. Hearing of these events, Re came in haste to see what had occurred. Shu and Tefnut cried and screamed and the cosmos fell into chaos. The gods and goddesses placed their arms on their heads, there was night without day, the sun disc became obscured and the earth became inverted, so that the rivers were unnavigable. The cardinal points fell into disorder and every being in existence, whether man or god, cried.

### Osiris' Body in Pieces?
Although there is no explicit reference in these mythological snippets to Seth hacking Osiris into many pieces, as recorded in later times by Diodorus and Plutarch, in the Pyramid Texts, there is mention of Horus collecting up the pieces of Osiris, seemingly after

Seth had dismembered him and thrown his remains into the Nile: 'I am Horus,' the inscription reads. 'I have come for you that I might purify you, cleanse you, revive you, assemble for you your bones, collect for you your swimming parts, and assemble for you your dismembered parts.' Additionally, some temples list parts of Osiris' body as being buried at different sacred sites; in particular, sometimes a piece is described as buried in each of Egypt's nomes. A New Kingdom papyrus that records myths concerning Osiris and Seth similarly mentions Osiris' body as broken into pieces and, in a later papyrus, Tefnut, Isis and Nephthys find the god's shoulder blade and tibia in a bush in Letopolis.

◄ CONCEIVING HORUS ►

When Isis found the body of Osiris (or had reconstructed it), she used her magic to resurrect him just long enough to become pregnant. How she resurrected Osiris differs depending on the source.

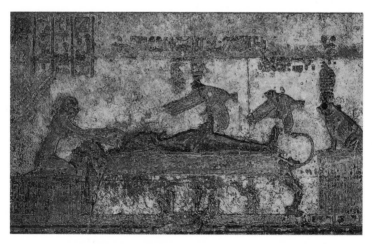

Hovering over the deceased Osiris, Isis, in the form of a kite, conceives Horus.

A late tradition at the Temple of Hathor at Dendera refers to Isis standing to the god's right and Thoth to his left. They place their hands on each part of Osiris' body, performing the 'opening of the mouth' ceremony (see pp. 170–71) in order to reinvigorate him (this ritual was practised by Egyptian priests over a mummy to 'awaken' the dead ready for their journey in the afterlife). Another tradition has Isis, in the form of a kite, flapping her wings to provide Osiris with the breath of life:

> *His sister was his guard, she who drives off the foes, who stops*
> *the deeds of the disturber [Seth] by the power of her utterance.*
> *The clever-tongued whose speech fails not, effective in the word*
> *of command, mighty Isis who protected her brother, who sought*
> *him without wearying, who roamed the land lamenting, not*
> *resting till she found him, who made a shade with her plumage,*
> *created breath with her wings, who jubilated, joined her brother,*
> *raised the weary one's inertness, received the seed, bore the heir...*
> THE GREAT HYMN TO OSIRIS, STELE OF AMENMOSE

The moment of conception was marked by a flash of lightning, which caused the gods to be afraid. Knowing that Seth would seek her out, Isis asked the gods to protect her unborn child in her womb, but Atum demanded to know how she could be sure that the child was a god. The goddess remarked that she was Isis and that the child was the seed of Osiris. This simple statement convinced Atum, who decreed that Seth should stay away from the pregnant Isis and that Werethekau (the 'great of magic'), a snake goddess, would guard against him.

◄ SETH STEALS THE BODY OF OSIRIS FROM THE WABET ►

Even after the body of Osiris had been reconstructed, there remained the need to protect it from Seth: at first, we are told, Nut spread herself over Osiris to conceal him from his enemy and even later on, when Anubis was mummifying Osiris' mummy (the process of embalming was one of the god's many duties), Seth continued to pose a threat. One day, when it was approaching twilight, Seth discovered the time that Anubis would leave Osiris' body alone in the *wabet* (the place of embalming). To evade detection, the trickster god transformed himself into Anubis and, just as planned, the guards failed to recognize him. Snatching Osiris' body from within the *wabet*, he sailed away on the river, carrying the corpse westward. But Anubis soon learned what had transpired and, along with the gods of his entourage, set off in pursuit. When they met, Seth took the form of a bull to intimidate the dog-faced god, but Anubis caught and tied Seth by the arms and legs, and severed his phallus and testicles. His enemy defeated, Anubis placed Osiris' body on his back, ready to return him to the *wabet*, and imprisoned Seth in a place of torture at Saka, in the 17th Upper Egyptian Nome.

On another occasion, Seth transformed into a great cat after again attacking the body of Osiris, but was captured and branded; these marks created the leopard's spots. Later, Seth again stole Osiris' body after transforming into Anubis (it was a good plan after all, worth trying more than once). As before, he was captured, but this time was sentenced to spend the rest of his life as a seat for Osiris.

Seth, perhaps unwilling to spend eternity as support for a corpse's buttocks, fled into the desert, pursued by Anubis and Thoth, who used his magic to fell him. Seth's arms and legs were bound, and the gods decided to burn him, hoping to be rid of him once and for all. The smell of burning fat reached the sky, 'and Re and the gods regarded it [the odour] as agreeable'. Anubis then flayed Seth, and wore his skin. In his macabre Seth-suit, Anubis rendezvoused with his enemy's followers, mingling with them on a mountainside until nightfall, when he put his violent plan into action. With a single swipe of his blade, Anubis severed their heads, leaving the blood from their decapitated corpses to dribble across the mountainside.

### Osiris and the Borgias

In 1493, Pope Alexander VI (Rodrigo Borgia) commissioned his painter Pinturicchio to create a series of frescoes in his private apartments at the Vatican. These included, among winged sphinxes and Nilotic palms, depictions of the myth of Osiris and of the sacred Apis bull. Although an unusual context for such pagan imagery, the subject matter was inspired by the creative work of Giovanni Nanni, secretary to the Pope, who had charted Pope Alexander's ancestry back to Isis and Osiris, and claimed that Osiris had brought Egypt's wisdom to Italy during his journey around the world. The family connection was strengthened by the presence of a bull in the Borgia family coat of arms; this was now reinterpreted as a depiction of the sacred Apis bull, which, by extension, associated the Pope with Osiris as instructor to mankind.

But Seth was not the only problem Anubis faced when mummifying Osiris: the process itself appears to have been too overwhelming for the god. One myth relates how the dog-faced god, distraught, transformed himself into lizards and scurried out of the *wabet* to tell people of the horrors he had seen within – probably Osiris' lifeless body. Hearing this news, all the gods became upset and wept.

◄ THE FUNERARY CEREMONIES OF OSIRIS ►

Once Osiris had been properly mummified, Re commanded a funeral be held for the fallen god. Anubis was to preside over the funerary ceremonies and Geb helped him to make the official arrangements. As the funerary procession sailed along the Nile, the mourners kept watch for the followers of Seth and at one point were attacked by reptilian creatures that transformed into cattle. The funerary cortège successfully evaded them, however, and continued on to Abydos where the funeral was held, Isis and Nephthys weeping throughout. Afterwards, festivities were held and the gods were pleased. To protect Osiris' body, Anubis surrounded the burial with snakes, called 'the gods who guard Osiris'.

◀ OSIRIS AS KING OF THE BLESSED DEAD ▶

Although Isis' magic revived Osiris long enough for her to conceive a son, the murdered god was not fully returned to life in the world of the living. Instead, Osiris' resurrection was confined to the Duat, where he ruled over the blessed dead as king. He was confined to this place and could only communicate with those in the living world through messengers. As the force of regeneration in the world, Osiris united with the ailing sun god in the middle of each night, filling him with enough energy to rise in the east each morning and continue his circuit. He also presided over the judgment of the dead, watching as the heart of the deceased was weighed against the feather of *maat* (see Chapter 8).

## THE REIGN OF KING SETH
## AND THE TRIUMPH OF HORUS

With Osiris dead, Seth ascended the throne of Egypt. The length of his reign differs depending on the source, but the Turin Canon gives him at least 100 years, while Manetho's *Aegyptiaca* – a Ptolemaic Period composition that now only survives as excerpted, sometimes manipulated, quotations in later works – gives either 29 or 45 years. During this time, Seth 'flooded the land with his evil designs', aided by his followers in the towns and nomes where his cult was strongest, particularly the 19th Nome of Upper Egypt and the 11th Nome of Lower Egypt.

Ramesses III is crowned by Horus (left) and Seth (right), divine rivals for the kingship.

One of Seth's first acts as pharaoh was to imprison Isis and Nephthys in the spinning house of Sais. There, Isis' heart became burdened and her eyes sunken from crying. It is unclear how long this incarceration lasted, but it was at least several months, as Seth assigned her work every 30 days. Other myths relate that Seth locked Nephthys in his own house, but she turned on him and escaped to assist Isis, leaving behind the son she had borne to her murderous husband. The identity of this son of Seth is unclear, though it is possibly Maga, an aggressive crocodile, who is said to have bitten off the left arm of Osiris. Maga's violent act and his subsequent denial of having swallowed the divine arm, led to his town being cursed and his tongue being cut out. Nephthys bore Seth further children, but harboured sexual passion for Osiris – perhaps one of the reasons Seth murdered his brother. For her betrayal, Nephthys lived in fear that Seth might kill her in retribution. Nevertheless, she still protected Osiris' body while hiding from her husband.

◄ HORUS' BIRTH AND YOUTH ►

**The Birth of Horus in the Papyrus Thicket**

> *O evil-doer [Seth], your crime is directed against you.*
> *Our lord is in his house and shall not fear. The child*
> *is greater than you. He will live and his father will live.*
> PAPYRUS MMA 35.9.21

When she finally escaped the spinning house, the pregnant Isis went into hiding in the northeast Delta at a place called Khemmis. According to the Greek historian Herodotus, this was a floating island at Buto (though he remarks that it wasn't floating during his visit). After ten months of pregnancy, Isis gave birth to Horus there. Unfortunately, Seth became aware of the birth because his bed shook at the moment of delivery and he awoke. Isis then raised

The hawk-headed god Horus wears the Double Crown of Upper and Lower Egypt.

Horus 'in solitude, his abode unknown' in the Delta marshes. As a youth, he was protected by Isis' magic, and various goddesses acted as his nurses and servants, including Nephthys, Wadjet and Nekhbet. Hathor, as a divine cow, served as Horus' wet nurse, as did Nephthys.

Seth went in search of the young Horus for many years, uprooting papyrus and burning the marshes in his quest, but Isis took protective measures to ensure that the angered king could not find him, gathering up Horus in her arms and moving on whenever she sensed Seth's destructive rage. On one occasion, Horus of Behdet (see box p. 56), who had sworn to protect Horus even before the child was born, arrived with his fleet to protect the child Horus and Isis from Seth and his followers. A great river battle ensued between the two forces and Seth transformed into a hippopotamus, but Horus of Behdet was ultimately victorious for he turned into a strong young man armed with a harpoon that he used to spear his enemy.

### Illnesses and Difficulties Faced by Horus in his Youth

Despite divine assistance, Horus the Child continued to encounter problems, troubled either by illness or dangerous creatures (for the wider context of these myths see Chapter 6). One problem he faced, however, is common to children (and adults!) throughout the world even today: nightmares. 'Come to me, my mother Isis!' he is recorded as saying. 'Look, I see something which is far from me, in my own city!' Isis replied:

> *Look, my son Horus. Do come out with what you have seen – so that your dumbness finishes, so that your dream apparitions draw back! A fire will leap out against the thing that frightened you. Look, I have come to see you that I may drive out your vexations, that I may annihilate all ailments. Hail to you good dream! May night be seen as day! May all bad ailments brought about by Seth, the son of Nut, be driven out. Victorious is Re over his enemies, victorious am I over my enemies.*
> PAPYRUS CHESTER BEATTY III

Physical pains also afflicted Horus; these were sometimes attributed to demons or worms. In several tales we find that these pains were specifically stomach aches. After eating a golden *abdu*-fish on the border of the pure pool of Re, Horus' stomach was in such pain that he had to spend the day lying down. On another occasion, Isis brought an *oip*-measure to purge the pain from her son's belly.

Pains sometimes entered Horus' body in the form of demons when suckling from his mother; one such demon caused his heart to become weary and his lips livid, so Isis, Nephthys and the weakened Horus went to visit men, maids and nurses to learn what they

had done in the past to cure their own children of similar possessions. At other times, the pain manifested in headaches:

> *Look, she has come, Isis there, she has come, swaying her hair*
> *like a mourning woman, she being of disordered appearance*
> *herself like the hair of her son Horus on account of the smashing*
> *of his head, of the ruffling of his side-locks by Seth the son of Nut,*
> *during the fight in the Great Valley!*
> PAPYRUS BUDAPEST 51.1961

Horus also suffered from burns:

> *Horus the Child is in the nest. A fire has fallen into his body.*
> *He does not know it, and vice versa. His mother is not present,*
> *who might conjure him.... The boy was small, the fire was*
> *powerful. There was no one who could save him from it. Isis*
> *came out of the spinning-house [at the] hour when she loosened*
> *her thread. 'Come, my sister Nephthys! ... Show me my way*
> *that I may do what I know [to do], that I may extinguish it for*
> *him with my milk, with the salutary liquids from between my*
> *breasts. It will be applied to your body so that your vessels become*
> *sound. I will make the fire recede that has attacked you!*
> PAPYRUS BRITISH MUSEUM 10059

Horus' problems could be less dramatic too: one myth recounts
how he cried out in his field because his cattle were being bothered
by wild animals, including lions, jackals and hyenas.

### Isis and the Seven Scorpions

Lengthier myths concerning Horus' youth follow similar themes,
the most detailed being the Myth of Isis and the Seven Scorpions.
In this myth, Isis escapes her prison, the spinning house of Sais,
and is visited by Thoth, who warns her of Seth's plans to harm her
child. He advises her to go into hiding until Horus safely reaches
adulthood and can challenge his evil uncle. Fully aware of Thoth's

reputation for wisdom, Isis and Horus leave that evening, carried within their palanquin and escorted by seven scorpions (manifestations of the scorpion goddess Serqet) for protection, three at the front of the palanquin, two within and two at the rear. The scorpions are instructed not to speak with anyone, whether noble or peasant, and to keep their faces down on the road, lest a message reach Seth before they can arrive at 'the House of the Crocodile' in the 'Town of the Two Sisters' on the edge of the Delta.

One day, as they journeyed, Isis, Horus and the scorpions approached a number of houses owned by a wealthy married woman, who spotted them from afar and ensured that all her doors were closed. This annoyed the seven scorpions, who decided to exact revenge. While Isis and the other scorpions rest in the home

---

**Isis and Horus in Christian Imagery**

With the conversion of the Roman empire to Christianity in the 4th century AD, cultural practices associated with the empire's pagan religions were assimilated, easing the adoption of the new belief system. In Egypt, however, Christianity had been spreading across the country since the 2nd century AD, allowing traditional, ancient Egyptian, ideas to penetrate the developing religion from an early stage. To Egypt's population, as well as to people of the Roman world in general, statues and depictions of Isis holding or suckling the child Horus will have been instantly recognizable thanks to the relatively recent growth of the cult of Isis throughout the Mediterranean, as well as the sheer antiquity of the iconography; consequently, whether via Copts or Roman converts, these may have served as the inspiration behind the iconography of the Madonna and Child – conventional representations that remain with us today. Similarly, images of the god Horus harpooning Seth in the form of a hippopotamus or crocodile (or indeed images of Seth slaying Apophis), representative of the defeat of disorder, were popular in the Roman Period, and perhaps inspired icons of St. George and the dragon.

---

Serqet in human form with the symbol of a scorpion upon her head.

of a peasant girl of the marshes, the scorpion Tefen, his sting now armed with the combined poison of each of the seven scorpions, scurried under the doorway of the rich woman's house and stung her son. It was as if a fire had broken out in her home and the lady began to lament and mourn. She could not tell if her son were alive or dead and wandered through the town crying, but no one came to her aid.

Isis became worried about the child, as she regarded him as blameless in the rich woman's selfishness. She called out to her, announcing that her mouth bears life and explaining that she was well known in her town for dispelling poisonous diseases with her words of power. Within the rich woman's house, Isis placed her hands on the boy and uttered the name of each of the seven scorpions in turn. By knowing their true names, Isis wielded power over them. She commanded their poison to leave the child and he quickly became healthy again. She then chastised the scorpions, reminding them that they were forbidden from speaking with anyone, and adding that they must refrain from discrediting their names in the districts. She then told them to keep their heads down until they could reach their hiding place at Khemmis. Witnessing these events, the wealthy woman saw the error of her ways and gave her possessions to Isis and the peasant girl.

## Horus Is Poisoned

With Horus safely hidden away in the mashes at Khemmis, Isis spent her days begging, gathering food to feed her child and looking after his needs. One day, however, she returned to find the young god unconscious. Tears from his eyes and saliva from his lips had moistened the banks of the river. His body was limp, his heart weak and he was unable to breastfeed. In panic, Isis called out to the local villagers of the marshland, imploring them to come to her aid, but none knew a spell to cure him. Then a woman came to help, a person of distinction in her district. She reminded Isis that Horus was safe from Seth in Khemmis, so the illness could not have been caused by him and suggested that she investigate Horus for any signs of scorpion stings or snake bites.

Leaning close to her child, Isis smelled the odour emanating from Horus' mouth and quickly realized what was wrong. Embracing Horus and crying, she screamed, 'Horus has been bitten, oh Re!' Her cries brought Nephthys and together they wept, the sound echoing throughout the marshes. Soon after, the goddess Serqet, arrived, asking Isis what was wrong and advising her to call out to the sky to catch the attention of the sun's barque: 'The crew of Re will come to a standstill', she said, 'and the boat of Re will not sail on as long as the boy Horus is lying on his side!'

Isis duly shouted to the sky, causing the sun disc to halt its progress. Armed with his magic, Thoth descended from the solar boat to investigate and, on meeting Isis and finding the sick Horus, he stressed the importance of Horus' safety to both himself and the other gods in Re's following. Isis was not impressed. 'Thoth, how great are your wits, but how slow are your plans!' she complained, telling him that there had been mishap after mishap, the number of which could not be counted. 'See, Horus is in distress on account of poison! The evil is a deed of my brother. Death is its final destruction.'

After listening carefully, Thoth calmed Isis, telling her not to be afraid: he had descended from the sky with the breath of life to revive Horus, he reassured her, and began to recite a lengthy spell that associated the protection of Horus with a series of divine beings, creatures and places. His words of power destroyed the poison, driving it from the child's body. Thoth then told the villagers to return to their homes and, at Isis' request, he cast a spell to prevent them from recognizing her true identity in future. Crisis averted, Thoth returned to the sky and the solar boat continued on its way, leaving Horus and Isis in safe anonymity.

### ◄ INCIDENTS OF RAPE AND INCEST DURING SETH'S REIGN ►

Just as Horus lived in fear of Seth's violence while growing up in Khemmis, his mother also faced considerable dangers. Isis suffered greatly at the hands of Seth, who robbed her of her possessions and sexually assaulted her on more than one occasion during his reign. One myth recounts how, after Seth had raped her in the 19th Lower Egyptian Nome, Isis became pregnant and gave birth prematurely; the child was born half-formed, as a black ibis merged with a baboon. On another occasion, Seth bound Isis and again attempted to rape her, but she gripped his penis with her vaginal muscles, leaving him unable to withdraw.

Leading a campaign against Seth, Isis transformed herself into the aggressive goddess Sekhmet and hid in a *gebel* (high rocky outcrop). From there, she sent out a flame against her enemies and burned them all to dust. Seth, however, spotted Isis and, recognizing her true identity, transformed himself into a bull to chase her down and sexually assault her. In turn, Isis changed herself into a dog, armed with a knife at the end of her tail. In this form, she managed to outrun Seth, leaving the aroused god to ejaculate onto the ground. Isis laughed at him, saying 'It is an abomination to have scattered [your seed], O Bull.' Leaving Seth behind, she changed into a snake and travelled to a mountain from where she could observe the movements of Seth's allies. As they crossed from the 19th Nome towards the Eastern Gebel, she stung each in turn, her venom penetrating their flesh. They died immediately and their blood spread across the mountain.

◀ THE RETURN OF THE KING ▶

*Horus has been untied from his breastband for you,*
*that he might catch those in Seth's following. Seize them,*
*remove their heads, sever their forelegs, and gut them,*
*take their hearts, and slurp their blood.*
PYRAMID TEXT 535

The conclusion to the myth of Horus involves the young god reaching adulthood and at long last confronting his uncle Seth, demanding the crown as rightful heir of Osiris. As always, there are many variations of the story, though the most detailed account, today referred to as *The Contendings of Horus and Seth*, is found on the New Kingdom papyrus Chester Beatty I.

## The Contendings of Horus and Seth

As one might expect, when Horus came to demand his crown before the Universal Lord, Re-Horakhety, Seth refused to abdicate in favour of his nephew and many of the gods supported his decision; others, however, offered their support to Horus, leading to a legal dispute that lasted 80 years.

Even from the outset, arguments were heated. Shu, an earlier king himself, said that the office of ruler should be awarded to Horus;

The god Banebdjedet.

the wise Thoth supported his decision, leading Isis to prematurely assume her son's success. She demanded that the north wind carry the good news to the West, so that it would reach Osiris in the Duat. Shu was pleased that Thoth had supported him, but the Universal Lord, presiding over the court, became angry at their presumptuousness, as he had not yet put forward his opinion.

'What is the meaning of your exercising authority alone by yourselves?' the Universal Lord shouted, and then sat in silence for a short time, furious at the Ennead. Sensing an ally, Seth intervened, asking that he and Horus be dismissed outside, assuring the god that his 'hands would prevail over his hands'; it seems that he wanted to settle matters with a fistfight.

Thoth, ever the diplomat, asked, 'Shouldn't we ascertain who is the imposter? Is the office of Osiris to be awarded to Seth even while his son Horus is still about?'

The Universal Lord became even more furious, he wanted to award the crown to Seth, but matters were descending into chaos. Onuris shouted out, 'what are we going to do?' and Atum suggested that the god Banebdjedet be summoned to the court to help judge the case. The court agreed and the god was sent for. Upon his arrival (along with Ptah-Tatenen, who seems to have hitched along for the ride), however, Banebdjedet refused to make a decision, and suggested that the gods write to the goddess Neith for her opinion on matters instead (and to do whatever she suggests). Accordingly, Thoth drew up a letter and sent it, asking what they should do. Luckily, Neith was more decisive than Banebdjedet, saying, 'Award the office of Osiris to his son Horus. Don't commit such blatant acts of injustice which are improper, or I shall become so furious that the sky touches the ground. And let the Universal Lord, the Bull who resides in Heliopolis, be told, "Enrich Seth in his possessions. Give him Anath and Astarte, your two daughters, and install Horus in the position of his father Osiris."'

Neith's letter reached Thoth while he and the Ennead were sitting in the 'Horus with the Projecting Horns' Court. Thoth read it aloud to his colleagues and together they declared Neith correct, but the Universal Lord again grew furious and vented his anger at Horus, telling him he was despicable, inadequate for the office, and had bad breath. Onuris became enraged, as did the Council of Thirty. The god Babi became so riled that he told the Universal Lord that his shrine was vacant, a particularly hurtful comment to a god because it implied that he had no followers. The Universal Lord, deeply offended and saddened, went to lie down for the rest of the day. The Ennead, also realising that Babi had gone too far, chastised the god, telling him to 'Get out!' before returning to their tents.

Hathor, the Universal Lord's daughter, came to stand before her father in his tent and unexpectedly exposed her private parts to make him laugh. Now cheerful enough to rejoin the Great Ennead, the Universal Lord asked Horus and Seth to each make a case as to why they should be king. Seth went first, pointing out that he was the most virile of the gods and that he slew Apophis – the enemy of Re – each night at the prow of the sun god's boat; no other god was able to do this, he added. The gods were impressed and proclaimed

Seth correct, but Thoth and Onuris reminded them that it is always wrong for an uncle to inherit the throne when the dead king's son lives. Banebdjedet, finally discovering his opinion, now sided with Seth, and the Universal Lord said something so shocking that it wasn't written down; whatever he said though, it affected the gods so intensely that they all became upset.

It was then Horus' turn to speak. He explained how wrong it was for him to be cheated in the presence of the Ennead and deprived of the office of his father. Unfortunately, he was not given much time to speak, however, as Isis interrupted him, exclaiming that the matter should be brought before Atum of Heliopolis and Khepri-in-his-Boat. The gods agreed with her and together told her not to become angry because 'the rights will be given to the one who is in the right'. This enraged Seth, who made an oath, stating that he would take his huge sceptre and kill a god each day, and wouldn't attend court, if Isis remained present. The Universal Lord, an ardent Seth supporter, decreed that the gods should sail to the 'Island-in-the-Middle' (perhaps in the Nile) to continue their hearing, leaving Isis behind. He banned the ferryman – the god Nemty – from transporting any woman to the island, expressly any that resembled Isis.

The gods travelled to the island immediately and, upon arrival, sat beneath the trees to eat bread. Meanwhile, Isis, not one to give up easily, transformed herself into an old lady with a stoop and a gold ring on her finger, and approached Nemty the ferryman, pleading for passage to the island. She told him she was bringing a bowlful of flour for a young man who had been tending his cattle there for five days and was hungry. Nemty was conflicted; he knew his orders, but saw only a harmless old lady standing before him. Isis reminded him that, really, it was only Isis he couldn't ferry across, and she was nowhere to be seen. She handed him a cake in return for passage, but Nemty wasn't impressed, so she offered him her golden ring instead. His greed now satiated, Nemty relented and took her in his boat to the forbidden island.

Isis arrived and found the Universal Lord sitting eating with his fellow gods. To attract the attention of Seth, she turned herself into a beautiful woman and immediately caught his eye. Seth followed her curiously and Isis told him she'd been the wife of a herdsman and had borne him a son, but when her husband died her son had been left alone to tend to the cattle. Then a stranger came and settled in their stable. He threatened to beat the son, confiscate the cattle and evict him. Isis turned to Seth and asked him his opinion of these events, adding that she wanted him to be her champion in these matters. The god, enraptured by this beautiful woman standing before him, did not hesitate: 'Are the cattle to be given to the stranger even while the man's son is still about?' He added that the imposter should be beaten with a rod in the face, evicted and the son put in his position.

Isis, pleased at trapping Seth, transformed into a bird and perched on the branch of an acacia tree, just out of Seth's reach. She told him to be ashamed, because he had condemned himself with his own mouth and his own cleverness had judged him. Breaking into tears, Seth ran to the Universal Lord, who agreed that he had indeed condemned himself. In retribution for allowing Isis onto the island, Seth demanded that Nemty be punished, so the unfortunate god was dragged into the presence of the deities on the island, and his toes were sliced off. From that day forward, Nemty hated gold.

At the insistence of Atum and Re-Horakhety the gods crowned Horus king, but Seth, enraged, challenged him to a duel. To determine the rightful king, he said, they should both change into hippopotamuses and plunge into the depths of the sea; the winner would be the god who could remain underwater for three months. As they sat underwater, Isis fashioned a harpoon and hurled it into the sea. Her first throw struck her son: horrified, she retracted the harpoon and aimed again for Seth. This time it found its mark, but Seth, calling on her to remember that he was her brother, persuaded her to release him. Horus felt betrayed. He emerged from the water, his face as fierce as an Upper Egyptian panther, and in a moment of rage beheaded his mother, who transformed into a headless flint statue. Taking his mother's head in his hands, Horus then disappeared up a mountainside.

The Universal Lord, furious at this act, decided that the gods had to punish Horus and so they ascended the mountain in pursuit of the young god. Seth found Horus lying in the shade of a tree and the two began to fight. Seth, much stronger than Horus, beat the son of Osiris to the floor before ripping his eyes out and burying them in the ground. Pleased with himself, Seth left Horus blind and alone, returning to his fellow gods and telling the Universal Lord that he had failed to find his youthful nemesis. While the gods continued to search for Horus, his eyes grew into lotus blossoms. Eventually, Hathor came across Horus, who was crying in pain beneath his tree. To heal him, she caught and milked a gazelle, pouring the milk into the god's empty eye sockets, so that they healed.

These acts of remorseless violence were too much for the gods of the tribunal. The Universal Lord told Horus and Seth to sort out

A statuette of King Tutankhamun harpooning.

their problems amicably over a meal or a jug of wine so that he and the other gods could have some peace. Acquiescing, Seth invited Horus to dine at his house, where they ate and drank and eventually went for a nap on Seth's bed. During the night, Seth became aroused and placed his penis between Horus' thighs. Surprised, Horus caught Seth's semen in his hands and ran to tell his mother what had happened. Isis cut off Horus' hands, throwing them into the river, and used her magic to manifest replacements. Suspecting that this was part of some larger evil design of Seth's, she aroused Horus by rubbing fragrant ointments onto his phallus and caught his semen in a pot. Then, carrying the pot of semen, she sprinkled Horus' semen all over Seth's garden, so that later that night, when Seth came to eat the lettuce there, he would become impregnated with Horus' semen.

Returning before the Great Ennead of the gods, Horus and Seth were again asked to present their cases. This time, Seth announced that he should be king because he had performed 'a man's work' against Horus. The Ennead cried out loudly and spat in Horus' face, but he laughed back at them. 'Everything that Seth says is lies', he said. 'Summon the semen and we'll see from where it answers.' Thoth came forward, and placed his hands on Horus' shoulders, saying, 'Come out, you semen of Seth!' The semen replied from some nearby marshes. He then placed his hands on Seth's shoulders, and said 'Come out, you semen of Horus!' The semen asked where it should emerge from and Thoth suggested Seth's ears; it then rose up as a golden solar disc. Seth became enraged and tried to grab the disc, but Thoth calmly took it from Seth's head and placed it upon his own as a crown. The Ennead announced that Horus was right and Seth was wrong.

Incensed, Seth again challenged Horus to a duel. This time he demanded a race using stone boats, saying that whoever won the race would also win the kingship. Horus duly built his ship out of cedar and plastered it to resemble a stone boat; no one noticed his deception. Seth, on the other hand, removed the top of a mountain and carved his ship from it. The Ennead lined up along the shore to watch Seth launch his ship, but as soon as it touched the water, it sank. Irritated and furious, Seth transformed into a hippopotamus and scuttled Horus' ship. In turn, Horus took a harpoon and hurled it at Seth, but the Ennead demanded he stop. Horus sailed his damaged ship to Sais to speak with Neith, complaining that it was time the judgment was finally made because the case had been dragging on for 80 years. Each day he had been proven the rightful king of Egypt, he grumbled, but Seth consistently ignored the Ennead's ruling.

Thoth then suggested to the Universal Lord that a letter be written to Osiris, so that he might judge between Horus and Seth. Distressed, Osiris wrote back, 'Why should my son Horus be cheated when it was I who made you mighty and it was I who created barley and emmer to sustain the gods as well as the cattle after the gods, whereas not any god or any goddess was competent enough to do it?' The Universal Lord was not pleased with Osiris' response and wrote back to him, saying that even if he had not been born, barley and emmer would still have existed. In his reply, Osiris decided to be more direct about his wishes. He raged that the Universal Lord had created injustice as an accomplishment and that justice had been allowed to sink down into the Duat. He then added a not so thinly veiled threat:

> As for the land in which I am, it is filled with savage-faced
> messengers who do not fear any god or goddess. I have but
> to send them forth, and they will bring back the heart of
> whoever commits misdeeds and they will be here with me.
> THE CONTENDINGS OF HORUS AND SETH

Thoth read Osiris' letter aloud to the Ennead, who quickly proclaimed him right, perhaps fearing for their hearts, but Seth again made a challenge to Horus, demanding that they go to the

Island-in-the-Middle to contend further. This they did, and Horus yet again overcame his uncle.

Matters had come to a head and the gods were no longer happy to watch Horus and Seth fight. Atum commanded that Seth be brought to him as a prisoner in manacles and asked him why he had kept himself from being judged and why he wanted to usurp the office of Horus. Seth, at long last, relented and told him to bring Horus and award him the throne of Osiris. Accordingly, Horus was brought and crowned, and Isis shouted in joy. Ptah then asked what should be done with Seth, and Re-Horakhety – the Universal Lord

---

### The Secret Name of Seth

Putting aside their differences, Horus and Seth went sailing together on Horus' golden barque. As the two gods sat enjoying their boat ride, an un-named creature crept across the deck towards Seth and bit him, causing him to fall ill. Like his mother during the incident with the secret name of Re, Horus asked Seth to reveal his true name so that he could use his magic to heal him.

'One works magic for a man through his name,' Horus reassured his evil uncle. Like Re before him, though, Seth was reluctant to give up his secret name so easily, even if it meant putting his own life in danger.

'I am Yesterday, I am Today, I am Tomorrow which has not yet come,' Seth said, but Horus knew better, saying that he was none of these things. Seth thought some more, before saying that he was a Quiver Full of Arrows and a Pot Full of Disturbance. Horus again disagreed. 'I am a man of a thousand cubits, whose reputation is not known, I am a threshing-floor, made fast like a bronze which a cow has not swept. I am a Jug of Milk, milked from the breast of Bastet.' Horus complained each time, until Seth finally relented: 'I am a Man of a million cubits, whose name is Evil Day. As for the day of giving birth or of conceiving, there is no giving birth, and trees bear no fruit.' Seth's true name finally revealed, Horus was able to cure the bite and the god was again able to stand.

---

– responded that he would take him to dwell with him as a son; he would thunder in the sky and be feared. The entire land and the Ennead rejoiced now that matters had finally been settled.

## Alternative Accounts

Other accounts of the confrontation between Horus and Seth are extremely brief. In the Pyramid Texts, Horus captures Seth and brings him before Osiris. Seth is then judged in the court of Geb for his violence against Osiris. Here Horus plays only a minimal role, as the case is judged between Seth and Osiris. It concludes with Osiris being awarded his kingdoms on earth and the sky, while Seth is punished by being forced to carry Osiris. Seth then works with Horus for the benefit of the dead king: they unite to slay a serpent and provide ladders for the king to ascend to the sky.

The Pyramid Texts also make repeated reference to the injuries suffered by Horus and Seth during their fighting. Seth's testicles,

The Pyramid Texts from the tomb of King Pepi I.

---

**The Eye of Horus**

Horus' loss of sight in one or both eyes, and their subsequent healing, is a theme in Egyptian religious texts representing the re-establishment of order after disorder. This is why, in temple scenes, the Eye of Horus, called the *wedjat,* is often offered by the king to the gods – it symbolizes the king's role in ensuring order and balance in the cosmos.

The manner in which Horus loses his sight changes depending on the version of the myth. Either one or both eyes are taken by Seth and destroyed or buried. In some cases Horus heals his sight himself, but more often he is aided by Isis, Thoth or Hathor.

The Eye of Horus is also mentioned in spells, predominantly those governing the healing of eyes: they tell of its creation (by the Souls of Heliopolis) or of Thoth bringing it to Heliopolis. The Eye of Horus often appeared on amulets for it was a source of protection for people: 'It spreads its protection over you, it fells all your enemies for you, and your enemies have indeed fallen to you... The Eye of Horus comes intact and shining like Re in the horizon; it covers up the powers of Seth who would possess it...'

As a sky god, Horus' eyes have celestial connotations too; his right eye was the sun god's night barque and his left eye the day barque, or sometimes his right eye was the sun and his left eye the moon. Indeed, the Eye was particularly associated with the moon; its waxing phase represented the slow restoration of the Eye, until it reached full health again.

---

symbol of his sexual potency, are brought back to him by a messenger, while Horus' eyes, representing his clarity of vision, are similarly returned. Even Thoth is injured: his arm has to be restored. In a further spell, Seth takes Horus' eye in the eastern side of the sky. The gods then fly across the Winding Waterway (see p. 119) on one of Thoth's wings to intercede on Horus' behalf for its return. Seth tramples Horus' eye and devours it, but Horus eventually takes it back through violence or petitioning. The Coffin Texts describe Osiris as squeezing off Seth's testicles for Horus and, apparently, according to a later source, a legal hearing was held in the Great Palace of Heliopolis concerning Horus' taking of Seth's testicles.

The New Kingdom *Great Hymn to Osiris* presents Isis as bringing Horus before the broad hall of Geb. The Ennead are jubilant at his arrival, welcoming him as heir of Osiris, and they crown him at Geb's command. The world immediately falls under his control and Seth is given to him, apparently to be executed – the 'disturber suffered hurt, his fate overtook the offender'. The world was now ordered again: 'Abundance is established by his laws, roads are open, ways are free, how the two shores prosper! Evil is fled, crime is gone, the land has peace under its lord.'

Similarly, in the Ptolemaic Period *Book of the Victory over Seth*, Geb presides over a court hearing, convened to decide who should be king of Egypt; Seth's crimes are reported during the proceedings and Horus (supported by Thoth) is given a verdict in his favour. He receives deeds of inheritance and is crowned king, while Seth is exiled to the land of the Asiatics. Another version of the tale, inscribed on the Shabaqo Stone, now in the British Museum, again

The Shabaqo Stone, carved during the 25th Dynasty.

presents events a little differently. Here Geb, acting as judge, separates Horus and Seth and forbids them from continuing to fight. He proclaims Seth the king of Upper Egypt and Horus the king of Lower Egypt, the dividing line sited where Osiris had drowned. Later, Geb changes his mind, however, and decides to award the entire country to Horus, since he is the son of Osiris.

### Plutarch's Version of Horus' Triumph

Just as Plutarch provides an account of the death of Osiris, he also records the myth of the triumph of Horus. He writes that Osiris returned from the dead to train the young Horus for his battle against Seth. Osiris asked his son what he thought was the most noble of all things, to which Horus replied: to avenge one's father and mother when they have suffered evil. Before the battle began, many of Seth's supporters defected to Horus' side, bolstering his numbers, and even Seth's concubine, the hippopotamus goddess Taweret, abandoned her evil partner.

Despite Seth's depleted numbers, the battle raged for many days until Horus finally prevailed. Captured, Seth was then brought to the young king in chains, but Isis refused to execute him, infuriating Horus, who removed Isis' royal diadem in his fit of anger; Thoth, ever a calm presence, simply replaced it with a helmet in the shape of a cow's head. Seth accused Horus of being illegitimate, but Thoth defended Horus and proved his right to the throne.

◀ SETH RETURNS TO POWER ▶

After Horus had ascended the throne, Seth attempted to regain power, taking control of the Delta and performing many sacrileges. During this time, Seth defiled temples, drove out priests, stole cult implements and divine emblems, damaged or destroyed temple property, uprooted and cut down sacred trees, caught and ate sacred

---

**The Wives of Horus**

Horus, son of Isis, is unusual among Egypt's gods because there is no clear wife associated with him. Myths typically present Horus as a bachelor, though magical spells sometimes assign him obscure wives, such as the Lady of the Cobra named Tabitjet, one of which was bitten by a snake or scorpion. In later times, Horus of Behdet (Edfu Temple) became the husband of Hathor of Dendera; their cults were connected and processions travelled between their two temples. At Edfu Temple, Maat is said to be a daughter of Horus.

---

animals and fish, blasphemed against deities, disrupted festivals, killed worshippers and stole offerings. Re was unaware of these acts until Isis shouted to the sky, yelling that Seth had returned without his knowledge. Ultimately, Horus was again victorious, and Seth was exiled.

◄ THE END OF THE REIGN OF GODS ►

With his final defeat of Seth, Horus ruled as king of Egypt for 300 years. He exacted revenge on anyone who had supported Seth, destroying their nomes and towns so that 'the blood of Seth fell in them'. Statues of Seth were destroyed and his name was removed from wherever it was found. 'Su mourns, Wenes is in a state of grief', we are told, 'moaning pervades Sepermeru, the Southern Oases and the Baharija Oasis wail, evil circulates within them. Heseb cries out, for its lord is not within it, Wadju is an empty place, and Ombos is destroyed. Their mansions have been demolished, none of their inhabitants exist, their master is no more.'

After Horus, the throne passed to Thoth, who ruled for 7,726 years. The kingship next passed to Maat, and then on to each of

11 demi-gods, who together ruled for a total of 7,714 years; these demi-gods had unusual names, such as '[…] Does not Thirst', 'Clod of the Shore', 'Possessor of Noble Women' and 'Protector of [Noble] Women'. Spirit kings (*akhu*) then ruled, grouped together into nine categories and connected with particular locations such as Hierakonpolis, Buto and Heliopolis. These were succeeded by the Followers of Horus and then by human kings. The unnamed, Predynastic kings of Upper and Lower Egypt were collected together as the souls of Nekhen and Pe, regarded as *bau* ('souls') of the Lower Egyptian city of Buto (Pe) and Nekhen (Hierakonpolis) respectively; those of Pe were shown with falcon heads, those of Nekhen as jackal-headed. These were powerful deities who assisted the king in life and death.

◄ THE PHARAOH ►

And so we reach the time of the historical pharaohs. In life, each king was Horus, sitting upon the Horus throne and possessing the inheritance of Geb. He was also the son of Re, acting as deputy to the sun god and charged with ensuring the stability of the world, just as Re had done personally at the beginning of time. The king might have been the product of the union of a human mother and a god, but he did not enter the ranks of the divine until his coronation. During this grand ceremony, the royal *ka* – the spirit of kingship – entered the mortal man's body and transformed him into a pharaoh. Through the coronation rituals, the man was reborn, his physical body infused with divine power.

This power, however, was limited by its human vessel, which continued to age and exhibit the same weaknesses as any other human. When a king died, the kingship continued on, inhabiting a new host with each death. In this manner, the king was not quite a god and not quite a human, instead he had his own sphere of

King Ramesses I is flanked by the souls of Pe (left) and Nekhen (right).

existence, below the true gods, but above mankind. His destiny was to act as intermediary between the two, pleasing the gods for the benefit of humanity, hoping to secure their divine benefactions. The king pleased the gods by ensuring *maat* existed throughout Egypt, by making offerings to the gods, by defending and expanding the country's borders, and by killing all enemies.

Despite his obvious human frailties and personal character, the king existed as a mythological figure. To posterity, his decisions were insightful and perfect, his appearance ever youthful and strong. Alone, he rode out at the front of the army, decimating his opponents, protecting his own troops from all danger. His acts were always successful, his behaviour pious and just. This ideal, mythological pharaoh, loomed large on every temple wall, smiting the enemies of Egypt or offering to the gods, his perfect deeds were inscribed on the walls of nobles' tombs and royal stelae. Though to history, the king as fallible individual was smothered beneath the finest linen cloak of ideology, the mythic pharaoh was ever-present and almost unchanging, a reassuring symbol of order in an unpredictable world.

# PART TWO

## THE LIVING WORLD
### (OR EXPLAINING THE WORLD AROUND US)

# THE MYTHIC ENVIRONMENT

The world of the gods and their mythology did not end with the transfer of the crown to human rulers: deities were manifest in, and oversaw, the forces of nature, so that an active mythology permeated every aspect of daily life. Myths grew up around settlements and natural features (see below pp. 130–34), often incorporating 'great gods' such as Osiris, Horus or Anubis, or centring on so-called 'minor' gods, deities that were predominantly local in character. There was a rich mythology of place, providing a history of the gods worshipped in the local temple, and an identity and character for the town and nome.

## ◄ THE GODS' RESPONSIBILITIES AND LIMITATIONS ►

Just like people, the gods had roles and responsibilities, jobs in the cosmos that only they could perform, as well as limitations. The gods of ancient Egypt were not omniscient and not omnipotent, but they could manifest themselves in different forms simultaneously, allowing them to remain in the sky or the afterlife realm of the Duat, while sending their *bau* – 'souls' or 'personalities' – to appear on earth. Through a god's *ba* or *bau*, you could feel his force, but the deity proper always remained distant. No matter what form they took, however, there were places that even the gods could not reach. On the whole, for example, the gods were unable to enter Nun, their authority ending at the limits of the created world. Even in parts of the Duat, in areas beyond the reach of the sun's rays, they had no power. Furthermore, the majority of Egypt's gods were limited by their associated town, area or region. The further an Egyptian

An early Ptolemaic Period conception of the Egyptian world. The inner circle
is Egypt, its nomes written in a ring around it. At the top of the outer circle is the cavern
from which the waters of the Nile originate. The goddesses of the east (left)
and west (right) hold the sun god's boat at sunrise and sunset respectively.

travelled from his home town, the less able his town god would be to
aid him. So, although a deity might be elsewhere, perhaps spending
time in the sky or in the Duat, he or she might only have authority
over a fixed geographic space on earth. For this reason, a traveller
prayed to the god of the region he was in, and if he did not know
what name to use, he would simply pray to the 'netjer', the word we
translate as 'god', though it means whichever force had responsibility over a particular space.

A god's responsibility was unique, a cosmic role in the created
world that no other deity could perform. Nut ensured the sky continued to exist. Shu's force kept the sky and ground separate. Hapy
governed the inundation's yearly occurrence. Osiris enabled new life
to spring from death – universal regeneration. The god Min ensured
fertility. Because each god's role was unique, if a god wished to
perform another god's function, the two had to 'inhabit' one another
– a process called 'syncretization' by Egyptologists, and described

as the gods 'resting' in one another by the ancient Egyptians. Gods were not all-powerful, and thus needed the 'force' provided by another god's responsibility to perform certain functions. So, for the god Amun to perform a fertility role, he and Min – god of fertility – inhabited one another temporarily to become Amun-Min, a new god who was at once both. Similarly, Amun, who embodied invisible and hidden power, might join Re – visible power – to form the all-powerful Amun-Re, the totality of visible and invisible power, the 'king of the gods'. In the middle of the night, the dying sun god joined with Osiris, to be empowered by his regenerative energy. The two gods then separated again, allowing the regenerated sun god to continue on his way into the dawn sky.

The gods Re and Osiris 'rest' in one another, flanked by Nephthys (left) and Isis (right).

### The True Appearance of a God

The living were unaware what a god really looked like: artistic representations only illustrated aspects of their characters. Hathor, for example, might be shown as a cow when her caring aspect was emphasized. If her angry and wild aspect were intended, she might be depicted as a lioness. Nobody expected the deity's true appearance to be in this form. Though a god's appearance remained unknown, his arrival could be felt in great natural disturbances, such as earthquakes and the sky trembling. The Cannibal Hymn relates: 'the sky is clouded, the stars are disturbed, the "bows" quake, the bones of the earth god tremble'. A god's appearance is also preceded by the smell of incense, by blinding radiance and by a presence felt in your heart. The impression is of a great formless, invisible force, unknowable and indescribable in its totality. This force, however, could be interacted with in a physical, tangible manner through vessels that the invisible god could inhabit, most often the cult statue at the back of a temple or shrine.

The goddess Hathor.

◀ THE CREATED WORLD ▶

At its simplest level, the created world – the world in which the Egyptians lived – as organized by Re at the time of his departure from earth, was divided into sky and land, and also included a third place, called the Duat (see pp. 123–24). Beyond the created world lay Nun, the infinite expanse of motionless and dark water that surrounded the earth on all sides. In this bubble of creation, the gods, the king, the blessed dead and humanity all existed as part of the same community.

Every aspect of creation had a divine explanation. The wind was a manifestation of Shu, for example, though he also encompassed the entire atmosphere: 'the length of the sky is for my strides, and the breadth of the earth is for my foundations'. The sky vault was the force of the goddess Nut, her consort Geb was the earth. Together, the physical manifestations of the Egyptian gods – their forces as principles of nature – accounted for all natural phenomena, though they themselves – their true forms – might be elsewhere. Through personification, the intangible forces of the gods gained form, allowing the Egyptians to interact with them. At the same time, the forces of nature, sometimes benevolent, sometimes destructive, were placed into an ordered system and assigned a named controller, who could be praised, cursed or begged for aid, depending on the situation. If your house blew down or was flooded, you had someone to blame. If a storm was coming, you knew who to beg to avert it.

◄ THE DAY SKY AND THE SUN ►

For an ancient Egyptian, stepping onto the dry earth (a manifestation of the god Geb) into the heat of the day (Re's life-giving power), he might feel a light wind on his face (the skin of the god Shu) and perhaps see an odd lonesome cloud (the bones of Shu) floating in the distance. And, so long as there wasn't one of Egypt's rare rainstorms (the efflux of Shu), he might stop for a moment to enjoy the wide expanse of the perfect blue sky before him. But how did he understand this imposing natural feature and the yellow ball that crosses it each day – not to mention its night-time counterparts?

The hieroglyph for 'sky' (*pet*) provides our first insight into the ancient mindset. It displays a flat surface, rather than a dome, with its edges downturned to make contact with the earth. The supports of the sky vault could also be depicted as columns or sceptres, which the pharaoh himself had the responsibility of securing. The god Shu, however, as the sky's main support, had since creation supported the goddess Nut, the sky vault, aided by the eight *heh*-gods, two to each of her limbs. (Apparently, Shu created these gods because he was weary of holding up the sky alone.)

It was Nut's divine responsibility to ensure that the sky remained in place, as her force was all that held back the waters of Nun above. This is why the sky appears blue – it is Nun's inert waters, eternally present above all mankind, repelled by Nut's force. This ever-present threat of a ceaseless deluge from above was a daily reminder of the disorder that is all around. Indeed, Nut acted more like an invisible force-field than a transparent wall; if you were able to fly up and reach the limit of the sky, you could put your hand through this force and touch the waters above, like dipping your fingers into a vast upturned ocean. You did not simply slam into an invisible barrier. For this reason, the sky could be sailed upon, and like on any body of water, this requires a boat. This is how the sun god – the force responsible for ensuring the sun disc's circuit each day – travelled from the eastern horizon to the western horizon: he sailed upon his day barque, called *mandjet.*

The sun was the creators' most visible and powerful manifestation; his light brought heat and growth, and enabled life to thrive, while wiping away the hated darkness. Its slow march over the horizon each morning was a sign that all was well in the cosmos. 'Fine gold does not match your splendour,' one sun hymn relates, 'through you do all eyes see, they lack aim when your majesty sets. When you stir to rise at dawn, your brightness opens the eyes of the herds.' As told in the myths of creation, this slow-moving ball of flame was the sun god's fiery eye, watching over his world as the hours passed until darkness fell. Although often a solar disc or a hawk-headed man in a boat, the sun god had other manifestations too. In the morning he was Khepri, shown as a dung beetle because of this insect's habit of pushing balls of dung along the ground, just as he rolled the sun disc skyward. At midday, when strongest, he became Re; at this time, when the sun appears to pause high in the sky (the Egyptian word for midday was 'ahau' also meaning 'stand-still'), Isis and Seth fought the chaos snake Apophis to protect Re; they were always victorious, so the solar barque could continue on its way. In the evening, the sun god became Atum, oldest of the gods, reflecting the sun's great age at the end of the day. When the sun took this form, his boat had to be dragged by jackals to its place of setting on the horizon of the western mountain.

Seth harpoons the chaos snake Apophis from the prow of the sun god's solar barque.

### The Aten

The Aten is the physical, visible sun disc, which radiates heat and light. It is known from the Middle Kingdom, but only became important as a god in its own right during the 18th Dynasty, culminating with the reign of Akhenaten (meaning 'He who is effective for the Aten'), when, for a short time, the Aten became the sole state deity. To Akhenaten, the Aten was a transcendent god, unlike the traditional gods, who were limited by time and space. Furthermore, the Aten could only be understood by the king alone: the rest of Egypt's population, including the priests, could only gain access to him through Akhenaten. Such a heretical approach to religion was not tolerated for much longer than Akhenaten's reign and under his son Tutankhamun the traditional cults were re-established.

The Aten, shown as a sun disc, shines its rays upon Akhenaten and his family. Each of the rays terminates in a hand.

◄ THE NIGHT SKY ►

At the end of each day, the goddess Nut swallowed the sun god, plunging the land into darkness. In the sun's last moments, as its rays vanished and its orb dipped below the horizon, the sky turned red, signifying a time of danger, and then black. The stars now sparkled, the Milky Way glistened, and the moon and planets charted their course through the darkness. A new world became visible.

Just as the earth featured areas of water and land, the night sky presented a similar terrain. The Egyptians envisioned the route that the sun, moon and planets followed through the sky as a 'Winding

Waterway', likening it to a river; this narrow band is today known as the ecliptic. The heavenly bodies' meanderings remained consistently within this band throughout the year, its extremes to the east and west marking its 'banks'. The Winding Waterway divided the night sky in two, with zones called the Field of Offerings to its north and the Field of Reeds to its south. To the north, also, were the 'imperishable stars', while in the south were the 'unwearying stars' – stars that never set below the horizon and so were always present. Some regarded the stars as decorations on the body of the goddess Nut, whose shape was seen in the Milky Way, her head the stars near the constellation of Gemini and her legs a division in the star pattern at Cygnus. Others saw the stars as the patterns on the body of the sky cow Mehet-Weret, 'the Great Flood', whose body was thought to be the Winding Waterway. The Book of Nut (a New Kingdom

The late Ptolemaic Period Dendera Zodiac shows the 12 signs of the zodiac and 36 decans; its content is highly influenced by Greek and Mesopotamian thought.

Constellations depicted in the tomb of King Seti I.

collection of sacred texts accompanied by an image of the goddess) describes the stars as travelling across the sky over the course of the night, just like the sun in the day, to be swallowed by Nut in the west. This violent act of consumption is said to anger Geb, who regards the stars as his children. Luckily, before Geb explodes with rage, Shu reassures him, 'Don't quarrel with her because she eats your offspring, they will live, they will go out from the place of her hindquarters in the east each day just as she bears [Re].'

The Egyptians divided the night sky into 36 decans, or groups of stars, which could be depicted on the ceilings of tombs and temples; each decan rose above the horizon just before dawn for a period of ten days each year. Certain constellations became associated with particular gods. The god Sah was the constellation Orion and husband to the goddess Sopdet (the star Sirius) whose appearance on the eastern horizon at dawn after roughly 70 days' absence heralded the annual inundation and the new agricultural year; this event was called 'the coming forth of Sopdet' (*peret sepdet*). Sopdet's connection to the inundation, and thus the renewal of agricultural fertility, is perhaps why she was sometimes regarded as a daughter of Osiris. The shape of Ursa Major, called Mesketiu by the Egyptians, was seen as the hind leg of an ox and associated with Hathor. Other constellations were 'Ape', 'mooring posts', 'Giant' and 'Female Hippopotamus', though these have not yet been identified in the sky.

Five planets, known as 'stars that know no rest', were noted by the Egyptians; each became associated with a god sailing in his celestial barque. Mercury was Sebegu, a god connected with Seth; Venus was 'the one who crosses' or 'god of the morning'; Mars was 'Horus of the Horizon' or 'Horus the Red'; Jupiter was 'Horus who Limits the Two Lands'; and Saturn was 'Horus, Bull of the Sky'.

◄ THE MOON ►

Once the sun had set, the moon took charge as its nightly replacement, acting as the sun god's deputy, a duty typically attributed to the god Thoth. Like the sun, the moon traversed the sky aboard a boat, but shined a weaker light upon the land. How could this be explained? And why did the moon change shape? Of the myths that surrounded the moon, most prevalent was that it was Horus' weakened left eye, as opposed to his strong right eye, the sun. Horus' left eye was damaged, typically by Seth, who was said to have torn it into six pieces, but was repaired, normally by Thoth, who restored it with his fingers or by spitting on it; this act of renewal was repeated each lunar month, as the moon slowly waxed until complete. For this reason, the moon was also called the 'one that repeats its form' and 'the old man who becomes a child'. The moon was also associated with Osiris, as the Egyptians saw the reconstitution

Anubis leans over the lunar disc in a posture familiar
from scenes of the god mummifying Osiris.

of his dismembered body – cut into 14 parts in this variant of the myth – in the nightly restoration of the moon's full shape. This was regarded as an act of rebirth: a stele from the reign of Ramesses IV greets Osiris, saying 'you are the moon in the sky; you rejuvenate yourself according to your desire and become old when you wish'. Funerary scenes show Anubis leaning over the lunar disc in the act of mummification, just as he is shown leaning over the deceased. Furthermore, because of the moon's association with Osiris, the sewing of crops was regarded as best done during a full moon. In its crescent form, the moon's shape appeared as the horns of a bull, an animal associated with fertility and power.

Various gods are connected with the moon; in addition to Thoth, most common are Khonsu and Iah. The god Iah's importance was later absorbed by Khonsu, who is best known as the son of Amun and Mut, completing their family triad (see box p. 24). Depicted for much of Egyptian history as a child wearing the sidelock of youth, with a lunar crescent and a full moon atop his head, in the Old Kingdom (when the Pyramid Texts were composed) Khonsu was presented as a vicious deity, who helped the king absorb other gods' strength by catching them and helping him to devour their bodies. As a cosmic deity, Khonsu could also be shown as a falcon-headed man. Sometimes, the lunar god in question is depicted at the centre of the full moon, otherwise the *wedjat*-eye – the restored eye of Horus – might be shown. Each of the 15 days leading to a full moon was presided over by a different god (Thoth first), who on each day performed the task of 'filling' it. The moon then waned for 15 days, as each of these gods, one by one, left the lunar 'Eye'.

◄ THE DUAT ►

The sun's journey during the night-time hours was a matter of great interest to the Egyptians. Where did it go? Would it rise again? Though traditions varied in the specific details of the sun's exploits

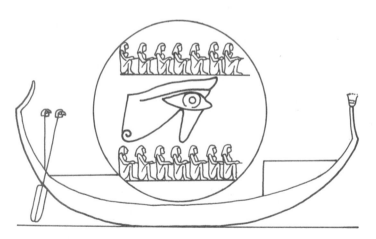

The 14 gods of the waning moon (excluding Thoth).

during the night, the overarching themes remained consistent: after passing below the western horizon, the sun journeyed through another part of the created world; this was the Duat, a dangerous location, full of demons and the dead, who attempted to assist or hinder the sun on his way to being reborn in the morning.

The location of the Duat is never well defined, though it is described as any place that is not sky or land. According to one custom, the sun spent the night within the body of Nut, gestating in her womb, ready to be born again in the morning, rejuvenated. Here and elsewhere in the textual sources, the Duat is located in the sky, somehow 'within' the body of Nut or within some invisible tunnel. In other cases, it is clear that the Egyptians regarded the Duat as underground. In one myth, the gods shout down into the ground to gain Osiris' attention, while snakes, living in the ground, were believed to have a special connection to the Duat. In offering rituals, the liquids used, such as water, wine and blood, drained into the ground to reach the dead and the gods of the Duat. Whatever its location, the Duat was certainly part of the created world, and so for this reason 'Otherworld', 'Netherworld' and 'Underworld' are unsuitable translations, for they lend it a sense of removal from the world around us that was not intended; indeed, 'Farworld' might be the most suitable English rendering. Like a distant land, the Duat was present in the created world, but only accessible to those who met one of two criteria: being dead or a deity.

## ◄ THE SUN'S NIGHTLY JOURNEY ►

Although the dead spent their time facing their own challenges in the Duat (see Chapter 7), the deceased king travelled with the sun god into the Duat each night and participated in his renewal. This renewal, however, was never guaranteed, for every night the sun god and his followers fought a great battle against the proponents

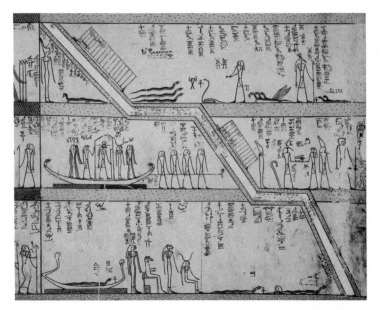

In the *Amduat*'s fourth hour, the desert of Rostau is crossed by a zigzagging path.

of disorder and the chaos snake Apophis. These events were spread over the 12 hours of the night, with the passage from one hour to the next blocked by tall gates, each protected by its own guardian, normally in the form of a fearsome snake.

So, each day, having grown weak, old and tired, the sun god descended below the western horizon towards a great gateway called the 'Swallower of All' – the entrance to the Duat. There, he was met by jubilant followers and welcomed by baboons. The god and his entourage, many in their own boats, then sailed along a watery expanse called Wernes, a place of abundance, where people wore sheaths of corn in their hair. Those who approached the solar flotilla were assigned land and provisions by the sun god.

After the gods had navigated the Waters of Osiris, in the fourth hour of the night, the Duat's landscape changed; the solar flotilla passed from a land of abundance and water to the dry desert cavern of Rostau in the 'Land of Sokar, who is on his sand'. The path through this scorched landscape zigzagged and was interrupted by fire and gates. Winged snakes with legs traversed the sands and the solar boat itself was forced to transform into a snake to ease its movement (but even so, Re's followers were still forced to drag it through the sands). In the fifth hour of the night, the solar boat entered the Realm of the Dead, where Isis and Nephthys protected the burial mound of Osiris, and the Lake of Fire burned the enemies of order, while purifying those that had lived just lives. The waters of Nun flowed through this terrain, carrying those that had drowned and never received a proper burial. In the sixth hour of the night, the solar boat approached a well brimming with the waters of Nun. The sun god's corpse, in the form of a beetle, lay in the water, where it united with Osiris. This was the key moment of the night; Osiris' regenerative powers now energized the weakened sun god, providing him with the strength required to begin his journey to the eastern horizon. The kings of Egypt lined up to watch and Thoth healed the solar Eye.

In the seventh hour of the night, Re, protected by the Mehensnake, defeated his enemies. Seth and Isis attacked the chaos snake, Apophis, while others, aided by the scorpion goddess Serqet, tied his body down. Having quashed the proponents of disorder, the sun's followers punished their enemies, and a snake-headed demon bound and beheaded the enemies of Osiris. The eighth hour now began, in which the victorious sun god provided garments for the (grateful) dead. Similarly, in the ninth hour, the sun provided cloth for the dead, while others brought grain to feed them. Here, too, the enemies of Osiris were punished, this time in a court of law.

With goddesses lighting the way, serpents upon their heads, in the tenth hour the solar boat arrived at '[The one] with deep water and high banks'. Inhabiting a rectangular pool of water, those that had drowned were saved by Horus, who provided them with

### Sokar

Originally a god of the Memphite necropolis, over time Sokar became strongly connected with the funerary sphere in general and with the Duat, presiding over his desert domain in the fourth and fifth hours of the night, as described in the *Amduat* (see below). Sokar could be depicted as a hawk-headed man, wearing the White Crown of Upper Egypt or Osiris' *atef*-crown. Occasionally, he is shown with a human face and wearing a lappet wig. Whether standing or seated, his body is normally wrapped in a cloak, and he holds a sceptre and a whip. Sokar could also be shown fully as a hawk wearing the Double Crown of Upper and Lower Egypt, and was closely identified with the *henu*-barque, a heavily ornamented ritual boat, perched upon by the Sokar falcon.

A statuette of the god Ptah-Sokar-Osiris.

The Pyramid Texts cite Sokar as the creator of the 'royal bones', who received the deceased king in the afterlife and then sent him into the sky aboard his *henu*-barque, helped by Horus; he also played a key role in the resurrection of the non-royal dead. Additionally, Sokar was originally patron of craftsmen, especially metalworkers.

Sokar often appears in a syncretized form as Ptah-Sokar-Osiris, who represents creation, metamorphosis and rebirth, combining each god's dominant power and responsibility. His family groupings are never fixed, so that although he has a female companion called Sokaret and a son called Reswedja, Nephthys and Seshat can each sometimes be cited as his consort. Sokar's divine grouping is also fluid: in Memphis he is grouped with a Memphite version of the god Khnum, Herremenwyfy and Shesmu, while in his solar form he is associated with Nefertum and five 'divine daughters of Re'.

The cavern of Sokar in the fifth hour of the *Amduat*.

a proper afterlife. In the eleventh hour, the gods prepared for the sun god's rebirth at the eastern horizon and the enemies of Re were annihilated, some immersed in pits of fire. Isis and Nephthys, in the form of snakes, took royal crowns to the city of Sais and a snake, called 'the world encircler', rejuvenated the sun. The gods now entered the body of this world-encircling snake, marking the onset of the twelfth and final hour of the night. Elderly figures dragged the solar boat through the snake's body, emerging from its mouth as newborn children. Dawn arrived and Khepri, the solar beetle, rejuvenated and young, flew towards the sky, raised up by the god Shu, who duly closed the Duat's gates behind him. The sun rose over the twin lion Ruty, and a new day began.

The preceding description is based on the *Amduat* '[The Book of] What is in the Duat', an afterlife text copied onto the walls of New Kingdom royal tombs. As time progressed, however, royal tombs were decorated with additional afterlife 'books', each presenting the sun god's trials and tribulations within the Duat in a slightly different manner. The Book of Gates, for example, places its emphasis on the gateways that the solar barque had to pass on its way to the dawn, and shows the ram-headed *ba* of the sun god, encompassed by the protective coils of the Mehen-snake, aboard his boat,

---

### The Pyramid Texts

Royal afterlife beliefs evolved over the three millennia of ancient Egyptian history, with the earliest known description of the king's posthumous destiny inscribed on the walls of the 5th Dynasty Pyramid of Unas at Saqqara. These inscriptions, today called the Pyramid Texts, were then inscribed in the pyramids of subsequent Old Kingdom kings and some queens. The inscriptions helped the king ascend to the sky and meet the gods, so that he might spend eternity accompanying the sun god and exist as an imperishable star.

He could reach the sky in a variety of ways: he might use ramps or transform into a grasshopper or be helped by the god Shu. To navigate his way successfully, the king needed to know the geography of the afterlife, and the dangers he might face. He spoke with gate guardians and the ferryman, and had to reveal the correct names and show the correct knowledge to proceed. The Pyramid Texts include many references to the king's provisions, movements and the repelling of enemies and forces, including snakes and scorpions. Some locations cited are familiar from later afterlife 'books', including the Field of Reeds and the Field of Offerings, while additional locations are cited, including the Lake of the Jackal, and the Winding Waterway. Once ascended, the dead pharaoh travelled across the sky in his boat in the sun god's retinue.

---

flanked by the gods Hu and Sia. The Book of Gates also includes a scene depicting Osiris' judgment hall between the fifth and sixth hours; here, a pig, as symbol of disorder, is scared away and invisible enemies lie beneath the god's feet. In the sixth hour, assistants carry the corpse of the sun god, but his body is invisible; contact with his flesh renders the arms of his carriers invisible too. In the seventh hour, the enemies of Re are tied to jackal-headed 'stakes of Geb', to be tortured by demons. In the Book of Gates' final scene, the sun is reborn from Nun, rather than raised by Shu. The Book of Caverns, unlike earlier compositions, places emphasis on the torture of the damned, while The Book of the Earth focuses on the role played by the gods Geb, Aker (a god who guarded the eastern and western horizons) and Tatenen in the solar resurrection.

◄ THE LAND ►

The ancient Egyptians viewed their country as a flat strip of agricultural land at the centre of a disc-shaped world; the black fertile soil of this terrain gave the country its most common name: *Kemet*, the 'Black Land'. The hieroglyph for 'land' reflects this, showing a flat strip of land, often with three circles below it, illustrating clumps of earth. Egypt's agricultural wealth led Osiris to play a major mythological role in the daily lives of its people; as a god who embodied the principle of regeneration, he was responsible for the growth of the crops each year. The land as a whole, however, was a manifestation of Geb, while the Memphite god Tatenen, who primarily symbolized the first mound of creation, could sometimes, by extension, represent all fertile land emerging from the receding inundation, and even Egypt itself.

The Egyptians divided their country into Delta and Nile Valley – Lower and Upper Egypt respectively – which were themselves subdivided into a series of administrative *sepauwt* (districts or provinces) better known today by their Greek name, nomes. Their number varied over time: by the later phases of Egyptian history there were 42 nomes, 20 in Lower Egypt and 22 in Upper Egypt. Each nome was identified by its own emblem and personified by its own goddess, shown with the nome emblem upon her head.

The deities within the major temples of each nome could either be unique, or local forms of major state gods, such as Horus. So, for example, in Upper Egypt, Thoth was the major god of the 15th Nome, with his centre at Hermopolis; Anubis of the 17th Nome; and Nemty of the 18th Nome. Over time, mythologies developed around

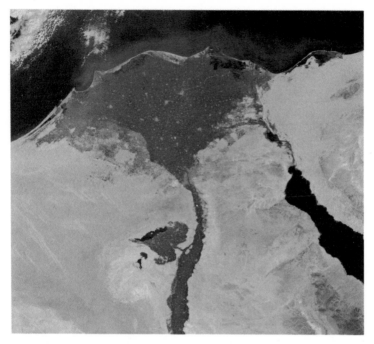

The sharp division between green agricultural land and harsh yellow desert is striking.

these deities, their nomes and temples: Papyrus Jumilhac records myths special to the 17th and 18th Upper Egyptian Nomes; a naos from El-Arish details myths of the 20th Nome of Lower Egypt; while Papyrus Brooklyn 47.218.84 collects together myths from a variety of Delta nomes, some of which are not known from any other source. Sometimes these myths were based on popular themes, adapted for the local environment; many temple sites, for example, claimed to be the original spot of creation – the first land that rose from Nun. From this foundation, they then adapted the general Egyptian conception of creation around their own particular deities.

Myths could also provide explanations for festivals. The local version of the festival of 'consecrating the sticks', held at Letopolis

---

**Greek Gods in Egypt**

The Greeks saw in many of Egypt's gods and goddesses equivalents of their own deities. These correspondences include:

Zeus = Amun
Hephaistos = Thoth
Dionysos = Osiris
Demeter = Isis
Typhon = Seth
Apollo = Horus
Hermes = Thoth
Aphrodite = Hathor

In turn, these associations led to certain Egyptian cult centres receiving Greek names, built around the Greek name of the god rather than the Egyptian: the cult centre of Thoth, ancient Khmun ('8-Town', after the Ogdoad of the pre-created universe), modern el-Ashmunein, was known as Hermopolis ('City of Hermes') to the Greeks; while a centre for Hathor, ancient Per Nebet Tep-ihu ('the House of the Lady "First of the Cows"'), modern Atfih, close to the Faiyum Oasis, became Aphroditopolis.

---

in the Delta, commemorated a time when Horus and Seth, along with their followers, fought each other in that nome; in the associated myth, while fighting their enemies – who have taken the form of birds – and capturing them in a net, Horus and his followers accidentally beat Osiris to death, as he is trapped in the net with them. In the festival, the consecrated sticks were probably used to beat symbols of Horus' enemies – probably birds – in nets.

These myths and associations were not unchanging; for example, by the New Kingdom, the goddess Bat of the 7th Upper Egyptian Nome had been assimilated into the cult of Hathor from the 6th Upper Egyptian Nome. Sometimes the traditions of a local myth crossed nome borders: the 'Osiris Books' recording the rites performed during his festivals and their dates, spread from their source in the 9th Nome of Upper Egypt to towns throughout the country.

Although all nomes had their own deities, and each temple developed its own mythology, normally based around certain 'core myths', some locations were more mythologically 'charged' than others. Gehesty – probably the site of Komir, near Esna in Upper Egypt – is where, according to the Pyramid Texts, Seth murdered Osiris. It is also mentioned in Papyrus Jumilhac as the location where Isis defended the body of Osiris from Seth by manifesting herself in various forms: becoming the lion goddess Sekhmet; a dog

---

**The God Nemty, in a Myth from the 18th Nome of Upper Egypt**
Often depicted as a hawk, Nemty, ferryman of the gods, and main deity of the 18th Nome of Upper Egypt, normally appears in texts as the unfortunate recipient of increasingly unpleasant punishments. We have already seen how, in *The Contendings of Horus and Seth*, Isis bribed him with gold to ferry her across to the island where Seth and the other gods had retreated. For this, the gods removed his toes, and he declared gold 'an abomination' in his town. Similarly, in another myth, Nemty was paid gold by Seth to ferry him across the river to the *wabet* to attack Osiris's body. This time, Nemty's tongue was apparently cut out.

Papyrus Jumilhac, a collection of myths from his nome, presents Nemty as having been flayed, seemingly for removing the head of a cow goddess in Aphroditopolis (even though Thoth used his magic to fix the cow's head back onto her body). His skin and flesh were removed because of their connection to his mother's milk, but his bones, associated with the semen of his father, were left untouched. The gods then went travelling, carrying Nemty's flesh with them. Nemty was bandaged up to replace his lost skin, but luckily for him, shortly afterwards the cow goddess Hesat (sometimes cited as the mother of Anubis), used her milk to regenerate his flesh. Such myths sought to explain why Nemty's cult statue was made from silver – the bones of the gods – rather than the customary gold – the flesh of the gods.

---

with a knife for a tail; and a serpent associated with Hathor. In this last form, we are informed, she went to a mountain in the north of the nome to watch the followers of Seth. When they descended the mountain she attacked them, poisoning them with her venom. Their blood fell on the mountain and became juniper berries. Another version of events in the same papyrus, speaks of Isis, with Nephthys at her side, transforming into a uraeus and biting her enemies and throwing lances at them. Gehesty is also where the gods are said to be buried; these include Shu, Osiris, Horus and Hathor of Gehesty, though later in Egyptian history many temples claimed to be the site of divine burials.

◄ THE NILE ►

Cutting through the eastern Sahara and flowing from south to north, where it joins the Mediterranean Sea, the Nile enabled life to flourish on its banks. For much of Egypt's length, the Nile is a single river, but at the point of modern Cairo and ancient Memphis, it breaks into many channels, forming the great marshland of the Delta; today, there are only two branches, but in ancient times there were five. This great divide between Valley and Delta, created by the Nile, fuelled the Egyptian obsession with dualism; the country could be referred to as 'the Two Lands', each represented by its own crown – the Red Crown for Lower Egypt and the White Crown for Upper Egypt. Furthermore, the goddesses Nekhbet and Wadjet came to represent Upper and Lower Egypt respectively. Nekhbet, meaning 'She of Nekheb' (the site of modern el-Kab), is normally depicted as a vulture and often wears the White Crown, while Wadjet was depicted as a snake wearing the Red Crown.

The most significant event of the year was the inundation of the Nile, a period of roughly three months (our July, August and September), when the river burst its banks and spread rich alluvium onto the land, perfect for growing crops once the waters had receded. This peculiar natural event was of constant interest to the Egyptians (and foreigners too), who sought to explain it. Over time, the annual occurrence became a symbol of cyclical rebirth, shaping the national psyche, fuelling mythology and reinforcing the Egyptians' belief that they were indeed blessed by the gods. One sign that the river was about to rise was the appearance of the star Sirius after an absence of about 70 days. Another was a noise emanating from a cavern beneath the shrine of the goddess Satet at Elephantine, the accepted source of the Nile at the country's traditional southern border: the gods propitiated Nun in this cave and even Re is said to have visited Nun there. To the Egyptians, all water entering the world came from Nun, and the Nile was no different – it was the 'high Nile' coming forth as 'fresh Nun'. The inert waters of Nun, inaccessible and infinite, completely surrounding the world, always threatened to break into and overwhelm creation; indeed, any time a hole was dug and groundwater was reached, that was Nun breaking in.

Although the Nile itself was not personified as a god, the inundation was referred to as the 'arrival of [the god] Hapy', and it

Tutankhamun's diadem, showing Nekhbet as a vulture and Wadjet as a cobra.

was through his action that fertility was brought back to the land. When depicted, Hapy typically has blue skin, a swollen belly and a loincloth. A clump of papyrus rests upon his head above his long hair and he has pendulous breasts – a sign of his fertility. He often carries a tray full of offerings. Like Nun, Hapy was thought to live in a cavern at Elephantine; however, 'no one knows the place he's in, his cavern is not found in books'.

Though Hapy lacked cult temples, Egypt's population praised him with hymns and music. He was the one 'who floods the fields that Re has made, to nourish all that thirst … when he floods, earth rejoices, every belly jubilates, every jawbone takes on laughter, every tooth is bared'. It was understood that all food existed because of Hapy's work, and that clothing and books could only be manufactured because his flood enabled flax and papyrus to grow. All herds were fattened because Hapy allowed crops to grow. Indeed, the bounty that followed Hapy's appearance was more precious than any treasure: 'no one beats his hand with gold, no man can get drunk on silver, one cannot eat lapis lazuli'. On the other hand, if Hapy made only a dismal appearance, chaos descended; everyone was poor, people died and fighting broke out.

The Nile inundation was also regarded as the tears of Isis, and the fluid that leaked from Osiris' corpse, spreading his regenerative force upon the lifeless soil, reviving and energizing it. When the waters receded, or whenever the Egyptians offered water to Osiris, it was regarded as entering Osiris' dead and dry corpse, bringing him back to life, just as the *ka*-spirit had to return to the body after death to reinvigorate the deceased.

The river was as dangerous as it was life giving; drowning was a frequent risk, while crocodiles and hippopotami dwelled in its depths, always ready to snatch people in their jaws and drag them to their deaths. For this reason, myths developed around the dangerous creatures that lived on the banks and in the river, and they became worshipped as gods, for example Sobek.

### Sobek

The crocodile-headed god Sobek with King Amenhotep III.

Typically depicted as a crocodile-headed man, Sobek wore a horned sun-disc and plumes, and is described in the Pyramid Texts as a son of the goddess Neith. Temples were built to him at particularly dangerous locations along the Nile, especially those where crocodiles might strike, such as at Kom Ombo in Upper Egypt, and in the Faiyum. As a god, he was associated with the riverbanks and the marshland, and in some sources the Nile was said to be his sweat. He also fished out Horus' hands from the Nile after Isis severed them (apparently, the hands kept slipping out of his fingers, so he became the first person to invent a net). Not content to dwell just in the river, Sobek was also called the Lord of Bakhu, a mythological mountain of the horizon, where he lived in a temple made from carnelian.

◄ BEYOND THE NILE VALLEY ►

The Egyptians regarded anything beyond the black, fertile soil of the Delta and Nile Valley as the desert, a place of disorder and danger, calling it *desheret*, the 'Red Land'. The abrupt separation between safe, life-giving greenery and savage, inhospitable danger was as striking to the ancient Egyptians as it is to people today. To the west were the yellow dunes and green oases of the Western Desert, while to the east were the mountains and hills of the Eastern Desert. Even further beyond lay lands quite unlike Egypt, where strange

Egyptian art presented people in standardized ways, for example their enemies (left to right): a Libyan, a Nubian, an Asiatic, a 'northerner' and a Hittite in Libyan costume.

people lived in a hilly terrain, contrasting with Egypt's level geography. Indeed, Egypt's natural borders, enclosed as it is by deserts to the east and west, the Mediterranean Sea to the north and the dangerous Nile cataracts to the south (now lost in Lake Nasser), fostered an attitude of invincibility and separation from the rest of the world. A mindset of 'them' and 'us' was enhanced by any invaders, or even peaceful traders, emerging as they did, shimmering and unannounced, from the hostile desert environment, products and personifications of its inherent danger, like sandstorms, snakes and scorpions – threatening Egypt's precious and pleasant cocoon. Consequently, images of the pharaoh smiting stereotyped foreigners became a symbol of royal (thus Egyptian) dominance, and of the world returning to its proper, ordered state.

It was in remote desert locations that the Egyptians sourced many of their natural resources. Turquoise could be found in Sinai, and gold and semiprecious stones in the Eastern Desert. Materials were often chosen because of the symbolic meaning of their colours: green was associated with life, prosperity and health; black with the Duat, fertility and rebirth. The veining of serpentine appears snake-like, and so it was used to make amulets and statues to fight against snakebites and poisons. Red stones symbolized human flesh, while gold was the flesh of the gods, and associated with the sun.

Certain materials were provided with divine, mythological origins. One myth records:

> *Horus cried and the water from his eye fell on the ground, it ran*
> *out and thus myrrh came into being. Geb did not feel well and*
> *blood from his nose fell on the ground, it ran out and became*
> *fir trees, and thus resin came into being from their sap. Shu and*
> *Tefnut wept bitterly and the water from their eyes fell on the*
> *ground, ran out, and thus incense came into being.*
> PAPYRUS SALT 825

A red mineral, found in the 18th Nome of Upper Egypt, was explained as blood-stained stone, left from a time when Anubis beheaded the followers of Seth on a mountain in the region. A myth from Bubastis refers to the blood of the goddess Bastet falling and becoming turquoise.

The desert lands were said to be have been 'given to Seth', but other gods were also associated with the desert. Often shown as a man or a hawk, Ash was a god of the Western Desert, with his

Desert cliffs in Sinai, land of turquoise.

responsibilities including the various oases and Libya. Ash also calmed the angry deities that opposed the deceased in the Duat. Another desert deity was Ha, identifiable by the three hills he wears upon his head, the hieroglyphic symbol for foreign lands. He is depicted armed with either a knife or a bow and protected people from danger in the Western Desert and at the oases, especially from nomads and Libyans. Since the sun set in the west, the Western Desert was closely associated with death.

Min and Hathor were thought to watch over desert routes; Min was associated with the Eastern Desert, but his main divine responsibility was sexual procreativity; his fertility is emphasized by his black skin, like Egypt's fertile black soil, and his erect penis, and he normally raises one of his arms – a threatening gesture, showing Min's power to protect. He was also believed to send rain clouds out into the desert. Sopdu, as Lord of the East, was similarly associated with Egypt's eastern frontier, protecting soldiers stationed at fortresses and mining outposts. When depicted as a man, he can be recognized by his long hair and pointed beard – the appearance of a Bedouin warrior. He is normally armed with a spear or axe, and wore a crown of tall feathers. He is also shown as a crouching falcon with a flail over his shoulder. The goddess Pakhet, 'she who scratches' or 'the tearer', was an aggressive goddess with responsibility for the entrance to *wadis* (dry riverbeds). Mines were connected with certain gods and goddesses too. At the turquoise mine at Serabit el-Khadim in the Sinai, members of mining expeditions prayed to Hathor, Lady of Turquoise, for protection; Hathor was also known as the Lady of Malachite, and, further, associated with gold and copper.

# DEALING WITH THE INVISIBLE
# IN DAILY LIFE

In addition to providing explanations for the physical features of the world around them, the mythological was imbued in every aspect of the Egyptians' daily lives. Myths accounted for falling ill, for good and bad days, and for dreaming. In this supernatural world, magic was a powerful everyday tool, employed to manipulate the environment and to ward off trouble, but its efficacy often relied on a grounding in mythical precedent. The mythic, the supernatural and the mundane, all were intertwined in the Egyptians' daily lives.

## ◄ MYTHOLOGY AND TEMPLES ►

It is 1200 BC, and you arrive at the great enclosure wall of the Temple of Amun at Karnak; its tall and grey rectangular shape, formed of mud-bricks laid in a wave pattern, looms above you, casting long shadows on the ground. Shielding the temple complex within, these walls mark a clear division between the hustle and bustle of the city, with its densely packed housing, squawking vendors and refuse strewn streets, and the pure sanctity of the god's house.

You pass into the grounds and see the sandstone walls of the Temple of Amun beyond, its entrance a tall pylon-gateway, flagpoles rising skyward at its façade, images of the king in the company of the gods carved deep into the sandstone. The pylon's sheer scale, far taller than any building near your home, invokes a sense of awe, and you praise the gods for favouring Egypt. All around, pilgrims scratch at walls with their fingers, wanting to take home fragments of the temple's divine power. Others rub statues of past nobles, who squat or kneel before entranceways like stone sentries, blankly gazing ahead as if petrified for eternity. Each of these wooden doorways temptingly leads into the sacred confines of Amun's house, but all are closed to you. Only on special occasions are they flung open and the public temporarily allowed inside the temple's sacred interior, and even then, only as far as the outer courts. There, privileged pilgrims meet further statues of Egypt's past elite, men given royal permission to place their statues within the temple courtyards, enabling them to take part eternally in the annual sacred festivals, to receive temple offerings and to be close to the god within. Today, however, it is not a special occasion; to enter the temple requires ritual purity, and not being a priest or a pharaoh – the highest priest in the land – you fail the test.

An Egyptian temple was not like a church or a mosque, it was not a place for the general population of a town or city to gather and pray on a regular basis: it was a god's house, his earthly palace, an interface between sky and earth, a representation of the cosmos. It was also a mythically charged zone: the enclosure wall served as a boundary between order and disorder, its wave-like mud-brick courses perhaps imitating the waters of Nun, lapping on the edge of creation. The pylon entrance represented the horizon, a place of transition between planes of existence, its twin towers the mountain peaks that flank the rising sun. The temple's straight axis mimicked the course charted by the sun across the sky. The hypostyle hall represented marshland, a transitional place where the waters of Nun gave way to the mound of creation. Its columns were the plants of this marsh, their capitals papyrus clusters or lotus flowers. Simultaneously, the columns served as pillars of the sky, an image re-enforced by the star pattern painted on temple ceilings. The god's sanctuary beyond, at the rear of the temple, was the first mound of creation, but also a representation of the sky, providing its divine occupant with familiar surroundings on earth. The different realms of creation were also built into the temple design: the ceiling and upper parts of the walls reflected the sky realm, the lower walls and floor the earth, and the crypts below the Duat.

Within his shrine, the god was manifest in his cult statue, formed of stone, gold, silver or gilded wood, and adorned with precious stones; he was not always present there, but could inhabit it whenever he wished, merging with this physical form so that the High Priest could interact with his previously invisible force. There, in the sanctuary, deep within the temple, priests performed rituals for the god at sunrise, midday and sunset (key moments in the daily life cycle of the sun, feeding him, clothing him and anointing him with fragrances), in the hope that he might perform good deeds in return. These were exclusive rituals, performed by a select few; only a deity's High Priest and the king could set foot in the sanctuary, those assisting in the rituals were relegated to the rooms and corridors outside.

The average person, then, was excluded from the gods in their temples, just as he was excluded from the king in his palace. The Egyptians required other means to build a relationship with the divine.

So how might you contact a god?

### ◄ CONTACTING THE GODS ►

The statues placed in the temple courtyard and in front of the outer gateways and doors served as one method for the average Egyptian to reach his deities. Some of these, whether depicting nobles or kings, served as intermediaries, passing on prayers from pilgrims to the gods inside in return for having their names and offering formulae read aloud. As one inscription, carved into a statue of the high official Amenhotep Son of Hapu, which once stood in front of Karnak Temple's tenth pylon, relates:

An inscribed statue of the high official Amenhotep, son of Hapu.

*O people of Karnak, who wish to see Amun. Come to me that*
*I may report your petitions. I am the herald to this god, as*
*Nebmaatre [Amenhotep III] has appointed me to herald what the*
*Two Lands say. Carry out for me 'an offering that the king grants',*
*summon my name every day like it is done for a praised one…*
EGYPTIAN MUSEUM, JE 44862

The devout could also enter special chapels 'of the Hearing Ear' built against the exterior back wall of temples (thus making them accessible at all times); within, large statues of the king and gods could be approached and petitioned. Divine images, carved as close to the sanctuary as possible on the outer walls of the temple, could also be approached; these images passed messages through the temple wall to the god in his sanctuary on the opposite side. Similarly, messages written on linen and attached to sticks could be inserted into the mud-brick walls of shrines or chapels, or into the temple doors or their frames. The god within might then read the message addressed to him.

Beyond the great walls of the state temples, small shrines dotted the Egyptian landscape. These were open to everyone, and often dedicated to gods who exhibited a particular influence over everyday life, such as Hathor, goddess of love, marriage and motherhood. At her shrine in Thebes, people left figurines of women or phalli hoping for fertility. Prayers of thanksgiving or penitence, inscribed on votive stelae, could also be left in sacred locations; if an individual believed that a god had intervened in his personal affairs, he might proclaim the god's power to the world in this manner. 'Ear stelae', inscribed with inscriptions and carvings of large ears, could also be left at shrines or in the vicinity of temples; acting like a sacred telephone, the divine ears gave the petitioner a direct line to a god or goddess, ensuring that he or she would hear all prayers and requests.

An ear stele from Memphis, carved during the New Kingdom.

145

### The God Imhotep

The god Imhotep.

Imhotep is one of only a handful of Egyptian gods who began life as a mortal, historical figure. As the designer of the Step Pyramid of Djoser, the first pyramid ever built, Imhotep lived and died under the 3rd Dynasty, but by the New Kingdom, over 1,000 years later, he was worshipped as the patron of scribes. By the Late Period, he was fully deified and prayed to for healing, so much so that the Greeks associated him with their own god Asclepius. Imhotep is perhaps best-known in modern culture as the mummy in the early Boris Karloff movies, and also in the more recent movies of the same name, starring Arnold Vosloo as Imhotep.

### Do-it-Yourself Egyptian Magic: Summon Imhotep

If you feel the need to summon Imhotep in a dream, follow these instructions, as recorded on a 3rd-century AD Greek magical papyrus, now in the British Museum.

1. Find a 'gecko from the fields'.
2. Drown it in a bowl of lily oil.
3. Engrave the words 'Asclepius of Memphis' (i.e. Imhotep) in Greek onto an iron ring that was once a shackle.
4. Dunk the ring in your expired-gecko lily oil.
5. Hold the ring up to the Pole Star.
6. Say seven times, 'Menophri, sitting on the cherubim, send me the real Asclepius, not a deceitful demon instead of the god.'
7. In the room where you sleep, burn three grains of frankincense in a bowl and pass the ring through the smoke.
8. Say 'Lord Asclepius, appear!' seven times.
9. Wear the ring on the index finger of your right hand while you sleep.
10. Wait for Imhotep to appear in your dream.

The sacred barque of Amun-Re, depicted within the temple of Seti I at Abydos.

### ◄ FESTIVALS AND ORACLES ►

On certain festival occasions, priests took their god's statue from within its shrine and placed it inside a portable shrine aboard its divine boat, usually stored in a room beside the sanctuary. Lifting the boat using poles flanking the vessel, and supporting the weight on their shoulders, the priests then carried the god in procession outside the temple. Throughout proceedings, the divine statue remained hidden from view behind a veil, secure inside the divine boat from the eyes of the impure. (One notable exception to this is the statue of the god Min, which appears to have been fully visible during his processions.)

On such occasions, typically involving a procession of the town's god, a local form of Amun or a deceased and deified king, such as Amenhotep I at Deir el-Medina, members of the public could approach the god for a consultation. They could elicit the god's opinion in a number of ways: the simplest was to ask a question, to which the god would provide his answer by inspiring the priests to tip his divine boat forwards for 'yes' or by making them step backwards for 'no'. Sometimes alternatives were presented – each written on a potsherd, limestone chip or papyrus. These alternatives were then placed on the ground in front of the procession for the god's divine gaze to peruse. In such cases, he would simply urge the priests to move towards the most suitable statement, 'taking' an answer. At other times a list could be read aloud in the presence of the god and his movement would indicate when to stop. Contrary to what one might expect, the gods' decisions were not always respected. One claimant during the 20th Dynasty argued his case before three different local forms of Amun, who nevertheless all confirmed his guilt.

Later in Egyptian history, temples had dedicated rooms where pilgrims could sleep in the hope of contacting a god in a dream, a practice called incubation. If you desired a cure for sterility,

---

**Dream Books**

If you preferred to sleep at home rather than at the temple, you could stay in your own bed for the night and visit the temple the next day to ask for your dream to be interpreted by a professional. Egypt's priests kept Dream Books, which recorded interpretations for a great many situations. 'If a man sees in a dream the god who is above,' one entry reads, 'good, it means a great meal.' Another states, 'If a man sees himself in a dream drinking wine; good, it means living according to *maat*.' Not all dreams were interpreted in a positive manner, however: 'If a man sees himself in a dream drinking warm beer; bad, it means that the suffering will come upon him.' Also, 'If a man sees himself in a dream removing the nails of his fingers; bad, [it means] the taking away of the works of his hands.' If you were too lazy to dream, you could pay a priest to dream for you.

---

for example, you visited the temple, slept the night, and the next morning described what you had seen to the dream interpreter. He then explained the best way for you to go about having a child. Perhaps the most important temple associated with incubation was that of Imhotep on 'the Peak' of Saqqara. In the Late Period, people prayed to Imhotep for medical help, and went to his temple to sleep and dream in the hope that this architect-turned-god would appear and cure them (or at least suggest a remedy). Nearby, a further incubation chamber was dedicated to the god Bes (see below); this was decorated with erotic imagery, and was perhaps where people went to cure their sexual or fertility problems, or even to give birth.

◀ CALENDRICAL MYTHS ▶

The Egyptian civil calendar was composed of three seasons, named after the agricultural events of the year: *peret* 'growing', *shemu* 'harvest' and *akhet* 'inundation'. Each season lasted four months, and each month lasted 30 days, broken into three ten-day weeks (called first, middle and last). Five extra days were added to the end of the year as the birthdays of major gods, known as 'epagomenal' days. In total, there were 365 days in the year. As a true solar year is slightly longer than this, the civil calendar and the solar year gradually fell out of sync, leaving the names of the seasons unconnected to the events they described. Thus, although new year's day (*wenpet renpet* 'the opener of the year') was celebrated at the beginning of the civil calendar, the Egyptians also recognized the heliacal rising of Sirius as the start of their solar, agricultural year. Because of the shifting calendar, this event only coincided with the same day in the civil calendar once every 1,460 years.

The seasons brought problems with them. The Nile was at its lowest in the hot summer months, and plagues, known as 'the plague of the year', spread throughout the country. Those that succumbed to the sickness were regarded as shot by the Seven Arrows of Sekhmet, a name given to minions of the goddess. From the 3rd century BC, Sekhmet's demons were led by the god Tutu, typically depicted as a sphinx. Through ritual action, the aggressive Sekhmet could be calmed and transformed into the friendlier Bastet, Hathor or Mut, in which form she might fight off pestilence rather than encourage it. People also used spells to ward off Sekhmet's plague. While walking around his house, holding a *des*-wood club, a man could recite, 'Retreat, murderers! No breeze will reach me so that passers-by would pass on, to rage against my face. I am Horus who passes along the wandering demons of Sekhmet. Horus, sprout of Sekhmet! I am the Unique One, the son of Bastet – I will not die on account of you!' This was just one of a great number of spells used to protect the home.

Equally dangerous were the five epagomenal days added onto the civil calendar after the last 'true' day of the year. This was a time of great danger and panic, when the Egyptians feared that the cosmos might grind to a standstill and the new year might never appear. On the last epagomenal day, it was thought that Sekhmet took control of 12 Messengers, murderers *(khayty)*, who came forth from the Eye of Re. Present throughout Egypt, they could see from afar, shoot arrows from their mouths and bring about slaughter through plague and pestilence. Understandably then, the arrival of New Year's day was a time of great happiness, when people celebrated by exchanging gifts.

Calendars of good and bad days associated each day of the civil calendar with a particular mythic event, and suggested to the reader the correct course of action to take on that day to avoid trouble or to achieve success. These events are sometimes presented in the present tense, as if their mythic activity is cyclical and ongoing, forever occurring on the same day each year. Many entries warn against leaving your home or eating certain foods or even going sailing; others warn against pronouncing the name of Seth on certain days.

For the 14th day of the first month of the *Peret* season, the entry in one calendar reads, 'Weeping of Isis and Nephthys. It is the day when they mourned Osiris in Busiris in remembrance of what they had seen. Do not listen to singing and chanting on this day'. For day 7 of the third month of *Peret,* we are told, 'do not go out of your house until Re sets. It is the day when the Eye of Re called the followers, and they reached him in the evening. Beware of it.'

#### ◄ GODS IN THE HOME ►

The vast majority of Egypt's population led a rural existance, living in mud-brick houses and ploughing the fields. Though in their great temples, deities were as inaccessible as the pharaoh in his palace, the gods and their mythology still played a prominent role in the home. This can be illustrated neatly thanks to the well-preserved remains of New Kingdom housing at Deir el-Medina, a state-run settlement built for the families of the craftsmen who cut and decorated the royal tombs in the Valley of the Kings.

Arriving back from Karnak Temple, perhaps after having watched a festival procession or after meeting with a priest to discuss his dreams, the craftsman enters his home through a wooden doorway, painted red to repel evil forces, and into the first of the four rooms of his thin, rectangular house. Set in a corner is a raised brick platform reached by steps – a shrine associated with fertility, decorated with images of the god Bes, dancing women and the con-volvulus vine, a symbol normally associated with 'birth arbors'. In both this room and the next, where a column holds up the ceiling and a low mud-brick bench provides a place to rest, rectangular and arched niches are set in the mud-brick walls; stelae and stone busts dedicated to ancestors – people regarded as 'excellent spirits of Re' – stand within. These sacred objects are worshipped by the craftsman and his family, who lay offerings on stone tables and place limestone

Ancestor busts, such as this one, were a link between the living and the dead.

bouquets of flowers before them to appeal for support from the recent dead. In the same two rooms, further niches contain miniature statues of state gods, including Sobek, Ptah and Amun ('of the Good Encounter'). Statues of household gods, such as Hathor and Taweret, stand in niches throughout the house, accompanied, like the ancestor busts, by stelae and offering tables. The craftsman's kitchen contains shrines to goddesses associated with harvest, such as Meretseger and Renenutet, and he keeps fertility figurines in his bedroom, to ensure a good sex life and the offspring that ensues. When performing rituals, the workman burns incense, regarded as the scent of the gods and called in ancient Egyptian *senetjer,* which literally means 'to cause to be divine'; its pleasant smell drifts through the air and, by inhaling it, the workman becomes closer to the deity invoked, allowing him to interact and commune with this invisible force.

In this confined mud-brick and stone space, the workman's life is played out: births; pleasant evenings with family and friends; quarrels; dreams, both unfulfilled and forgotten; nightmares; aging; and death. Through it all, his time on earth is dominated by the presence of the gods and their mythology. He prays to them when in need; he takes solace and inspiration from how they overcame the troubles they faced and continue to face; he is reassured by their daily presence in each room of his home, invoking their benevolent forces to influence the unpredictable melody of this largely indifferent, sometimes hostile world. Indeed, their favour fights the indifference, enables mastery over hostility. He does not believe this, he knows it to be true. After all, the gods' involvement in human affairs neatly explains many of the mysteries of everyday life: how is each individual formed? Where do we go when we sleep? Why do we get sick? Who decides when we die? Why do some live a long life while others die young? What is now mythology, was once explanation.

The goddesses Taweret (left) and Meretseger (right).

### Popular Household Gods

### Bes

The god Bes is unusual in Egyptian art because artists painted him face-on, looking at the viewer. He displays leonine features, with a mane and tail, and stands with his hands on his hips. His legs are dwarf-like, and a tall feathered crown rests upon his head. Bes' name probably derives from the word *besa*, 'to protect', as his divine responsibility was to scare away demons. In particular, he protected children, pregnant women and those giving birth, and also warded off snakes. To invoke Bes' help, the Egyptians painted or carved his image on household objects, especially bedroom furniture.

The god Bes.

### Renenutet

Renenutet, often depicted as a rearing cobra with a sun disc and horns atop her head, or as a snake-headed woman, had the power to nurture the fields and the young, encouraging them to flourish. For these reasons she was worshipped as a goddess of motherhood, fertility and harvest, and regarded as a divine nurse. She also protected the king and could destroy his enemies with a single glance. In later Egyptian history, Renenutet became associated with destiny.

### Mafdet

Mafdet was a violent protector, depicted as an African mongoose. She used her claws and teeth to attack and decapitate her enemies, especially those of the sun god Re. This aggressive nature was harnessed by the Egyptians in their daily lives. They depicted her on magical items and invoked her name in spells, notably to ward off ghosts. Despite helping the living, Mafdet was not quite so welcome to the dead: in the judgment hall of Osiris, she sometimes appears as punisher of the damned.

**Taweret**

Taweret, often called Ipet until the end of the Middle Kingdom, was another important household deity. She is a fearsome hippopotamus with pendulous breasts, a round belly and the arms and (rather stumpy) legs of a lion. Her tail and back, however, take the form of a crocodile. Upon her head, she wears two plumes on a modius (a flat-topped and cylindrical crown) and a sun disc. She often holds a *sa*-symbol of protection and an *ankh*-sign of life, and sometimes even a knife. In their daily lives, the Egyptians wore amulets of Taweret to ward off evil powers, and she was frequently depicted in the home during childbirth. She was also illustrated on beds and carved onto headrests to protect sleepers.

---

◄ BIRTH AND FATE ►

As our craftsman would have been well aware, the gods played a key role in life from the moment of conception. Some Egyptians believed that Ptah crafted humans and gods, forming deities from precious stones and metals, and mankind from mud or clay. Others regarded the ram-headed god Khnum as the deity that shaped gods, humans and animals; to them, Khnum span a lump of clay on his potter's wheel and, from this, moulded each person along with his *ka* (his double or life-force).

Magic was used at the moment of childbirth to protect the child, especially from female ghosts, who were thought to present a particular danger. Bes and Taweret helped to repel these spirits, though other deities were specifically connected with the birthing process, such as Heket, Meskhenet and Shay (see box pp. 156–57). When the time came for the mother to give birth, no knots were allowed in the house, whether for tying the father's kilt or the mother's hair, because knots were magically thought to constrain birth. Papyrus Berlin 3027 bears 'Magical Spells for Mother and Child', to be recited by a Lector Priest (see below p. 159). One of these repels demons who might hurt the baby, others relate to stopping illnesses and safeguarding the mother's milk. Some spells were meant to be read at dawn and sunset, and then the following sunrise and sunset. Demons harmful to the new child were warded off with garlic and honey, regarded as bitter to the dead, while everyday objects used by the child, such as cups, could be decorated with images of Taweret gripping knives and Bes holding snakes: fearsome scenes used to deflect evil.

Thoth decided the length of a person's lifetime, while a person's ultimate fate was decided at birth and announced by the Seven Hathors. In the New Kingdom *Tale of the Doomed Prince*, these goddesses announce that the prince will die by crocodile, snake or dog, while in the *Tale of Two Brothers* (also from the New Kingdom), they warn that Bata's wife will be killed by 'an [executioner's] blade'. In the 1st-century AD *Tale of the Doomed Prodigy Child*, a father is told that his son will die, 'at the age of sleeping with a woman'. Gods had the power to change a person's fate, however: Amun 'prolongs a lifetime, and he shortens it. He adds to the duration fixed by destiny on behalf of the one whom he loves.' It was also thought that Meskhenet determined status and that Renenutet decided material wealth.

---

### Gods of Birth and Fate

#### Heket

The goddess Heket, shown as a frog or frog-headed, was regarded as a female counterpart to Khnum, and is sometimes referred to as his wife, though she is also cited as the wife of Horus the Elder, as well as of the god Heh. Connected with childbirth, her image was carved into apotropaic wands (also called birth tusks) of the Middle Kingdom, and amulets in her shape were worn in the New Kingdom.

The god Khnum shaping a man on his potter's wheel.

### Khnum

Khnum was depicted with the head of a ram, sometimes with a plumed *atef*-crown on his head and a tripartite wig. Along with his wife, Satet, and his daugher Anuket, he was worshipped at Elephantine, at the traditional southern border of Egypt, from where he controlled the inundation of the Nile. The silt deposited by the inundation formed clay, and led to the belief that Khnum shaped all creatures, including human beings, from clay on his potter's wheel. He was also said to create all plants, flowers and fruit, and even ensured that quarries were filled with precious stones.

### Meskhenet

In ancient Egypt, women gave birth squatting, balancing on bricks. The goddess Meskhenet presided over birth as the personification of these birthing bricks; for this reason the unusual symbol shown on her head has been interpreted as a stylized cow's uterus. However, she could instead be depicted with a birthing brick on her head, or as a brick with a woman's head. Meskhenet was sometimes regarded as helping to determine a child's fate. Similarly, she could be present at the deceased's weighing of the heart ceremony (see p. 194), standing close to the scales that would determine his or her fate. Thus, she was not only present at birth, but also at rebirth.

### Shay

Shay, the personification of destiny or fate, is rarely depicted, but when he does appear, he is shown in human form, with a curved beard, though sometimes as a snake. Only known from the 18th Dynasty onwards, he was venerated throughout Egypt as a positive force, a protector, who represented the positive influence of the gods on a person's life; Shay came about through the creative will of a deity. His opposite, Nemesis, a form of divine retribution, was personified as Pa Djeba, 'The Requiter'.

◄ SLEEP ►

When unconscious, such as when asleep, a person was regarded as being in a condition similar to death. Sleeping, you might awaken in a dream, an alternate state of reality, in which you enjoyed a heightened perception, making it possible to witness events unfolding in distant locations – even as far as the Duat. This new condition was metaphorically regarded as a place existing somewhere between this world and the Duat, from which both the living and beings normally invisible, such as the gods and the dead, could be watched, though not interacted with. Thus, you did not dream as an action, rather you closed your eyes and awoke in the dream state.

Though a person might encounter a god in a dream, there was the fear that while unconscious, demons or ghosts might enter the bedroom uninvited, sometimes even sexually assaulting a person; they could also terrorize a sleeper in his dreams. For this reason, images of Bes and Taweret were placed around the bedroom, and used to decorate headrests. Vulnerable parts of the house might also be associated with gods, for example the doorbolts might be assigned to Ptah, while the four noble ladies, normally at the four corners of a sarcophagus, would be called on to protect the four corners of the bed. The Egyptians placed a uraeus (rearing cobra) of pure clay with fire in its mouth in each corner of the bedroom, to fight off nightmares and demons. Special stelae, used to ward off snakes and scorpions and to heal those attacked by them, were hung from walls. Even King Amenhotep III's bedroom at Malkata in Western Thebes was protected with images of Bes, while the ceiling was painted with the goddess Nekhbet as a vulture with her wings outstretched.

Seth created the elements from which nightmares were born. To scare away such night terrors, magical rituals could be performed, which served as protection from all evil forces that might 'sit upon' a person. (The idea of a demon sitting upon a person during the night is found across the globe, and describes the feeling of being paralyzed or crushed during sleep-paralysis and nightmares. In Chinese culture, for example, a ghost is thought to press upon the body, while in some Muslim countries, it is interpreted as caused by evil *jinn*. In Egypt today, on the West Bank at Luxor, such beings are called *qabus*.) In these spells, such as those in 'The Book of Driving out Terrors which come in order to descend upon a man in the night' (now P. Leiden I 348 v.2), a person associated himself with various gods, such as Atum, or played the role of Horus. Gods, such as Osiris or Sia, could also be called upon for assistance. Demons were told to turn away, so that the evil eye could not fall upon the sleeper.

◀ MAGIC AND MYTHOLOGY ▶

Magic, in one form or another, thus played an important role in the daily life of the Egyptians. In its most basic form, individuals used amulets of Bes or Taweret to ward off evil forces, and the majority of the population probably knew simple spells to influence the world around them as they went about their daily business. For more complex problems, however, it was normal to call on a professional: a Lector Priest – a person learned in the magic texts – who would arrive and perform powerful rituals.

Because of their special powers, Lector Priests are frequent characters in literary tales. They reconnect severed heads, turn wax animals into true animals, part the seas and animate clay men. In reality, they were learned, literate individuals, associated with the temples, who had access to a vast corpus of spells and conducted their magic in a rather peculiar manner: by intimidating the gods. If called upon to perform a ritual, the Lector Priest would announce that he had power over the gods and that they should do as he wished or else he'd bring back chaos: 'The sky will no longer exist, the earth will no longer exist,' one spell reads, 'the five days that complete the year will no longer exist; the sun will no longer shine, the inundation that comes at its time will no longer rise.' Simultaneously, the priest completely associates himself with the gods, announcing, for example, that he is Horus, or he is Thoth; by becoming fully absorbed by a god, the priest would gain the same influence that the divine possessed over the cosmos.

Many mythological references are found in Egyptian spells. By connecting the present situation, often an illness, with a mythological precedent, the spell gained authority – the idea being that if the spell benefited a god in the past, it would be just as beneficial in the present. Often, a spell derived this mythological authority from tales of Isis and Horus the Child when they were hiding from Seth (see pp. 86–87); one such spell, meant to relieve bodily pains, identified the sufferer with Horus, before detailing the instructions for its magical remedy:

> *Let these nine[teen] signs be made with the cutting-edge of a*
> *two-barbed harpoon; [to be provided(?)] with pellets of barley,*
> *drawn in fresh ink, to be applied to the affliction you suffer from.*
> *He will leave as a fart from your behind! This spell is to be said*
> *over [name], drawn in fresh ink on the belly of a man, on the*
> *sore spot on him.*
>
> P. LEIDEN I 348

Certain mythological accounts of Horus the Child being poisoned or stung, or needing protection from snakes and scorpions, are recorded on stelae known as *cippi*. These stelae were covered in magical spells and depicted Horus the Child holding dangerous animals and standing on the backs of crocodiles. The ritualist poured water over the inscriptions, which ran over the spells and absorbed their power. The water was then drunk, so that the magic entered the body.

Horus the Child, grasping various dangerous creatures.

## ◄ DEMONS AND GHOSTS ►

Because ghosts and demons were thought to cause illness, magic was also used to fight them off and people wore amulets of Sekhmet to repel them. Garlic, gold, spit and beer, as well as the more unusual gall-bladder of a tortoise, were also regarded as effective against demons and ghosts. Behaving more as emissaries for important gods, demons were usually dispatched by their divine masters to perform specific tasks, such as punishing cultic infractions. They inhabited locations that served as a connection between the Duat and the living realm, such as pools of water (where one might find a malevolent demon called a *weret* 'a great one'), tombs and caves. Demons are normally depicted as knife-wielding snakes, crocodiles or bulls with human bodies, while others could be more terrifyingly evoked, such as Shakek, 'whose eyes are in his head, whose tongue is in his anus, who eats the bread-of-his-buttocks, his right paw turning away from him, his left paw crossing over his brow, who lives on dung, who the gods in the necropolis fear'.

'Wandering demons' (*shemayu*) and 'passers-by' (*swau*) could cause infectious diseases, but demons could also be sent by the gods to possess people. In the Demotic *Tale of Inaros*, Osiris sends the demons Strife-Lover and Horus-Nemesis to 'create strife in the heart of Pimay the younger, the son of Inaros, against Wertiamonniut, the son of Inaros'. They enter into Pimay while he sits at festival with 40 of his men, causing him to forget the festival and suddenly want to fight, wrongly believing himself to be inspired by the god Atum.

Ghosts were also a source of trouble for the living. As one text, The Instruction of Ani, reads,

> *Appease the spirit, do what he likes, refrain from what disgusts him; may you be preserved from his many misdeeds, for every form of harm comes from him. A beast led away from the field? It is he who does such things. Damage on the threshing floor in the fields? 'It is the spirit' one says again. Tempest in the house? Hearts estranged? All that is his doing.*
>
> THE INSTRUCTION OF ANI

Ghosts, both friendly and malevolent, like demons, were an accepted part of the mythic landscape of ancient Egypt; interaction with the dead was an expected part of life. Ideally, at the end of each week, a person from an Egyptian household brought food and drink to the tombs and graves of ancestors at the cemetery. During the Beautiful Festival of the Valley, held annually at Thebes, families went to the necropolis to dine in the tomb chapels with the dead, leaving offerings at tombs, either for ancestors or renowned individuals. Though on the fringes of the settlement, the dead remained part of the community eternally.

If a person wished to communicate with a deceased individual, he could write a 'letter to the dead'. Such compositions were often written in ink on the inside of offering bowls and left at the tomb; once the deceased had consumed the offerings, he couldn't help but notice the message left for him. Using this cunning technique, the living could ask for help from their dead parents (including in their message reminders of favours done in life as not-so-subtle guilt-trips), or blame the deceased for problems. Indeed, if a person suspected that the malignant influence of a dead relative was behind recent troubles, he could even threaten to take up the matter with the court of Osiris in the Duat. In some cases, a recently deceased person could be contacted in order to reach an individual that had been dead much longer.

In the Egyptian conception of the world, it was the *akh* – 'transfigured spirit' or 'blessed dead', who had passed Osiris' judgment – that came closest to the modern meaning of 'ghost'. *Akhu* had unrestricted access to all parts of the created world and if they wished could 'haunt' the necropolis; they regarded the tomb as their home and could be summoned against enemies. They might also enter a person's house, cause nightmares and create trouble if irritated. Those who failed to reach the judgment hall of Osiris (who died violently or young, were executed by the state, or had not received proper funerary rituals) were, however, classed as *mut* '(unjustified) dead'. These were the worst form of evil dead, and are sometimes referred to as 'the damned'. Like the *akhu*, they could also cause trouble for the living, and were thought to take children away from their parents. The Egyptians also feared 'enemies' and 'adversaries', names given to groups of divine invaders from the Duat, who could enter the land of the living to intimidate and cause problems. Such beings could occupy a person's body, causing sickness and bleeding, or use their influence to generate problems. In particular, an entity named Nesy caused fever. Such belief in contact with the dead was not shared by all Egyptians, however, as the famous Harper's Song relates: 'None comes back from there [death], to tell of their state, to tell of their needs, to calm our hearts, until we go where they have gone!'

A number of tales relating the activities of ghosts have been preserved, though many are fragmentary. In the Tale of Petese, for example, known from fragmentary Demotic papyri and probably composed in the 1st century AD, Petese, a priest of Atum, encounters a ghost in a tomb (or its courtyard) at Heliopolis, while (perhaps – it isn't clear) searching for a wise man to cure his illness. The two walk hand-in-hand and the ghost laughs as they talk, but, irrespective of how well they are getting on, when Petese asks the ghost how long he has left to live, he is simply told to complete his years on earth. Angered, Petese casts a spell on the ghost and again demands to know the remaining length of his life, but the ghost only says that it is impossible to say. Changing tack, Petese decides to use the ghost as an intermediary between himself and Osiris, hoping that the king of the blessed dead might be able to provide some answers. But Petese's insistence on getting his answers and his refusal to leave the god's presence until he does so, enrages Osiris, and the ghost finally relents, telling him that he only has 40 days left to live – apparently a divine punishment for stealing gold and silver that belonged to Isis. Distraught, Petese returns home to tell his wife the bad news (then sleeps with her), and spends the next five days of his increasingly short life arguing with his fellow priests for 500 silver pieces – probably compensation for their role in his misfortune – to pay for his burial; as before, he eventually gets his way. He then creates a group of magical beings, charged with helping him to write down 35 good and 35 bad tales, one bad and one good for each remaining day of his life. These are not made to entertain him in his dying days, but as a gift from Petese to posterity. After Petese's death at the end of his remaining 35 days, he is buried, and his widow makes offerings to Re. The sun god then speaks to her in Petese's voice, so that his words directly enter her heart. Although the remainder of the tale is fragmentary, it is possible that it ended with Re resurrecting Petese, so that he was reunited with his wife.

In the Demotic *Tale of Setna-Khaemwaset and the Mummies* (copied onto P. Cairo 30646 in the early Ptolemaic Period), Prince Setna encounters three ghosts – Prince Naneferkaptah, his wife Ahure and their son Merib – in the Memphite necropolis while searching for the magical secret scroll of Thoth. In life, Naneferkaptah had discovered this secret scroll in a chest at the bottom of a lake in Coptos, but in doing so had incurred the wrath of Thoth, who prefers to keep his secret scrolls secret. To punish the plunderer, Thoth sent a slaughtering demon to cause him, his wife and child to drown in the Nile. And afterwards, although Naneferkaptah was taken to be buried in Memphis, his wife and son were interred in a tomb at Coptos, forever separating the family's physical remains.

Dismissing the ghost's tale of woe and ignoring the potential for angering Thoth, Setna demands that Naneferkaptah hand over the scroll, but he refuses, asking instead that Setna win it fairly from him over a board game. Setna duly loses each game, and with each loss, Naneferkaptah takes the game board and hammers Setna into the ground, until only the top of his head can be seen. His situation getting desperate, Setna calls for help from his foster brother, who brings magical amulets that enable him to fly up from the ground and steal the scroll out of Naneferkaptah's hand. In retribution, Naneferkaptah ensures that misfortune follows Setna wherever he goes, so that eventually the humbled prince returns the scroll to the tomb. As an act of penance, Setna travels to Coptos to retrieve the bodies of Ahure and Merib. He finds their mummies beneath the southern corner of the house of the chief of police and brings them back to Memphis, to be interred with Naneferkaptah, reuniting the family.

**Do-It-Yourself Egyptian Magic: A Spell for Exorcising Spirits with Beer**

As well as being a staple of the Egyptian diet, beer – whether 'sweet', 'stale' or 'of special offering' – could also be mixed with other items (often milk, oil or wine) as part of a magical prescription; whatever the mixture, the concoction was normally left over night before being drunk. So, to 'drive out suffering' from a man's stomach, ricinus seeds or fruit could be chewed and swallowed with beer. Magical papyri could also be soaked in beer until dissolved and then drunk with water, allowing the spells to enter the body. It was not always necessary to drink the beer though: a mixture of ground garlic and beer could be sprinkled around the house or tomb to ward off ghosts, snakes and scorpions during the night. The demon drink could also be used to exorcise a person of ghostly possession. So, if you need a good excuse for wanting that one extra pint at the end of the night, announce yourself demonically possessed, buy your drink and teach your friends the following spell:

> This ale of Horus [in] Khemmis which was mashed in [the town of] Pe, which was mixed in [the town of] Dep – drink it foaming! The sem-priest is standing up at his duty. You are the creation of the trapper who vomited Znst-plants, laudanum and lotus-flowers. Do drink the beer – it is to drive out the influence of a male or female dead that is in this belly that I have brought it…
>
> PAPYRUS HEARST [216] 14: 10–13

# PART THREE

## THE MYTHOLOGY OF DEATH
(OR EXPLAINING
THE LIFE HEREAFTER)

## THE TRIALS OF THE DUAT
## (A GUIDE)

The Egyptians had a complex view of the individual, in which a person was not simply a singular soul in a physical body, but multiple elements, each with their own distinct *raison d'être:* the *ka* represented the person's life-force and vitality; the *ba* was personality and movement; the shadow existed alongside the body in life, but was independent after death; the heart served as the seat of thought and consciousness; the name was fundamental to a person's identity; and the physical body was an image of, and vessel for, the person. These corporal and spiritual building blocks were integrated into the whole and were incapable of operating alone, at least during life.

◄ DEATH ►

*You sleep that you may wake; you die that you may live.*
PYRAMID TEXT 1975B

At death, when the body was deprived of the 'breath of life', the component parts of the individual separated. The person as a unity disintegrated, but the fates of the multiple parts remained entangled; the loss of a single element of the individual meant the second death of the whole, so all had to be cared for and protected. The *ka* remained perpetually in the tomb, requiring sustenance to survive, while the *ba* flew to the afterlife realm of the Duat, to exist in a transitional phase between physical death and judgment, travelling from its point of entry to the judgment hall of Osiris. The body, as

The four-legged, winged snake that represents Death, on the left.

an integral part of the deceased's personality, had to be preserved in order for the individual to remain whole. For this reason, the Egyptians developed mummification, re-enacting the procedure conducted by Anubis over the dead Osiris. In addition to the physical practice of mummification, putrefaction was warded off with magic, its destructive character personified as 'that slayer ... who kills the body, who rots the hidden one, who destroys a multitude of corpses, who lives by killing the living'. Incidentally, there is only one known depiction of death personified: on the Papyrus of Henuttawy (BM 10018), 'Death, the great god, who made gods and men' is shown as a winged, four-legged snake, with the head of a man and a tail terminating in a jackal's head.

By preserving the body, the Egyptians ensured that their spiritual elements had a vessel to return to – a place to recharge and renew. Statues inscribed with the deceased's name served a similar purpose, acting as backups in case the body became unrecognizable or destroyed. The heart remained in the body, the only internal organ to be left in place, as it was needed at the final judgment: without his heart, the deceased had no chance of joining the ranks of the blessed dead.

Once preserved, the body had to be made habitable for the *ba* again. This necessitated a ceremony called the 'opening of the mouth', which enabled the deceased to recover his functions, allowing him to eat and drink (despite being dead); these rituals reconnected the separated aspects of the person and 'reanimated' the body, ensuring his continued existence. He could now receive food offerings from the living – from relatives coming to spend time with the ancestors on festival days or indeed any person who happened to be wandering by the tomb chapel and be tempted inside. If physical offerings could not be brought, tomb inscriptions, listing items of food and drink, could serve as a viable substitute, magically manifesting a veritable post-mortem feast by their very existence on the tomb walls.

An 'opening of the mouth' ceremony for the mummy of Tutankhamun (left).

The *ba* was typically depicted as a human-headed bird.

But not only could the deceased now eat and drink, he could also speak; this was particularly helpful for his *ba*, flung into the Duat after death and questing on a journey to be judged, as he had to recite magical spells and announce the names of the dangerous denizens of the Duat in order to gain power over them. The repetition of the deceased's name by the living also increased his chance of survival; this is why, in tomb inscriptions, the name is found again and again. One instance of the name might fall with some loose plaster and shatter on the ground, but not hundreds; there was safety in numbers.

◄ ENTERING THE DUAT ►

*I arrive at the island of the Horizon-Dwellers, I go out from the holy gate. What is it? It is the Field of Rushes, which produced the provisions for the gods who are round the shrine. As for that holy gate, it is the gate of the Supports of Shu. Otherwise said: It is the gate of the Duat. Otherwise said: It is the door through which my father Atum passed when he proceeded to the eastern horizon of the sky.*

BOOK OF THE DEAD, SPELL 17

A dangerously armed denizen of the Duat.

### Gods for the Deceased

### Anubis

Anubis' main responsibility among the gods was to guard the necropolis and oversee the embalming of the deceased – a role that he first performed for Osiris. He also brought the dead before Osiris for judgment. His female companion is consistently said to be Input, but his parentage differs depending on the source; he is cited as a son of Osiris and Nephthys, or of Bastet, or even of Seth. Some sources cite Qebehut as a daughter of Anubis, fathered with the 'king's sister'. A celestial snake, Qebehut ('She of the Cool Waters'), assisted in the resurrection of the deceased and poured water from the four *nemset*-jars to purify the heart.

### Tait

Tait was a goddess of weaving, who provided the bandages to wrap the mummy and also wove the curtain of the tent of purification. In the Pyramid Texts, she clothes the king, guards his head and gathers together his bones. The deceased often wishes to wear clothes weaved by Tait, perhaps a loin-cloth.

### The Four Sons of Horus

Though referred to as sons of the god Horus, these four gods – Duamutef, Qebehsenuef, Imsety and Hapy – were also *bau* of the god. They protected the internal organs of the deceased, which were each placed in individual canopic jars and stored beside the mummy in a canopic chest.

The Four Sons of Horus protected the deceased's viscera, stored in canopic jars.

You close your eyes. You breathe your last breath. The world descends into darkness. Your heart stops beating. You open your eyes. You are no longer lying in bed, surrounded by weeping loved ones, but standing in a vast desert before a tall gateway. You are now in the Duat, a word often translated as Netherworld or Underworld, but which, in reality, referred to a place that was just as much a part of the created world as anywhere you might visit when alive, it was just simply out of reach of the living. From consulting your Book of the Dead, buried with you in your tomb during your funeral and now magically accessible, you know this to be the start of an adventure, rife with challenges, which could quite possibly end with your own second death – your obliteration from existence. To the Egyptians, physical death was not true death, just a change of circumstances; true death occurred in the Duat at the hands of demons or ordered by Osiris for those who had lived an unrighteous life.

Despite the anxiety that the thought of this encounter with the Great God might create, it was still a long way off. First of all, the many challenges of the Duat had to be overcome before you could even come close to Osiris' judgment hall. And the Duat itself was not a place to linger. It was a miserable place, the Book of the Dead relates: a desert, with no water or air, deep, dark and unsearchable, where there was no love-making. Traversing the Duat might not be particularly pleasant – it would surely be a brutal and harrowing experience – but staying still wasn't much of an option. Only by facing its trials could you reach the judgment hall and, having been assessed by the gods therein, be accepted as one of the glorious, transfigured dead, who appeared as divinities and were allowed free movement throughout the created world. How you then chose to spend eternity was entirely up to you.

So, you stand, newly arrived beneath the Holy Gate on the Island of the Horizon Dwellers at the start of your long and dangerous journey. Looking eastward, orientating yourself, you notice that the sky rests on top of a mountain. Your handy Book of the Dead (travel guide for the afterlife!) tells you this is the mountain of Bakhu. According to the text, the mountain is 300 rods long and 150 rods broad, and Sobek, Lord of Bakhu, lives on the eastern side of the mountain, where he inhabits a temple made of carnelian. On top of the mountain lives a snake called 'He who is in his burning', 30 cubits long; his first 8 cubits are made of flint and his teeth gleam. In fact, this snake has a glare so powerful that it can stop the sun god's sacred boat and can even swallow 7 cubits of the sacred waters. Luckily, on such occasions, the Book reassures you, Seth hurls an iron lance at the snake, causing him to vomit up all that he has swallowed. Seth then places the snake before him and says, 'Get back at the sharp knife which is in my hand! I stand before you, navigating aright and seeing afar.'

Given the Book's description, you look towards the top of the mountain and decide it best to keep your distance. But where to go now? The Book of the Dead provides some of the answers, citing key inhabitants and geographic features, though never including a true map; instead it only presents the different locations' relation to one another, or the time taken to travel between them.

### ◄ MAGIC IN THE DUAT ►

As in life, you are also aided by magic in the Duat; the Book's spells enable you to assimilate the character of the gods, providing you with divine authority, and thus the ability to repel enemies, stop yourself from being restrained, fight off putrefaction and even to save yourself from decapitation. To ensure that you are fully stocked with magical ability, the ferryman of the dead is sent out upon your arrival to sail upstream to the Island of Fire, to collect magic from wherever it might be found, all for you to use.

**A Map of the Duat: The Book of Two Ways**

Although not included in a Book of the Dead, maps of the Duat did appear during the Middle Kingdom. They were painted on the inside of coffins and were part of a composition called The Book of Two Ways.

This presents the sun god travelling from east to west on a blue waterway, and then passing along a dark path through the outer sky from west to east. Both ways were separated by the red 'Lake of Fire of the Knife Wielders'. The map shows locations, such as Thoth's Mansion in the Place of Maat; a mansion of Osiris; structures and tall walls of flint or flames; waterways; and shrines. Some places were to be visited, others were to be avoided.

Throughout, the land was populated by knife-wielding demons who attempted to block the deceased's progress. These demons had fearsome names, including 'Dog-face, whose shape is big...'; 'He who is hot'; 'Long-face who drives off aggressors...' and 'He who swallows; he who is alert'. In the Book of Two Ways, the

The Book of Two Ways, painted on the inside base of a coffin.

deceased uses magic to pass these demons and reach Rostau, 'the necropolis', a place 'at the boundary of the sky', where Osiris' corpse is 'locked in darkness and surrounded by fire'. Here he finds a hall divided by three walls of fire, and passes through them to reach paths of confusion. The deceased then travels with Thoth and becomes identified with Re, sailing in his boat. After passing through (usually) seven gates, he reaches Osiris and offers him the 'eye of Horus'. The deceased, now identified with Thoth, then spends eternity watching Re deliver a speech about his mighty deeds.

## How to Find Your Way

Apparently, it is enough to know the names and descriptions of the demons and locations of the Duat to make progress, especially as the gods and spirits themselves are meant to prepare a way through the dangerous terrain for you. With this knowledge you can be assured of reaching Osiris.

Knowing the names of dangerous traps is also helpful. Spells 153A and B of the Book of the Dead are illustrated with a giant net stretched between the sky and earth by fishermen, who also happen to be 'earth gods, the forefathers of the Swallowers'. In this net they hope to catch you during their attempts to halt those unsuitable to enter the next life. By reciting the spell, you announce that you will not be caught like the inert ones or wanderers: you have power over the net because you know its constituent parts, and also its name: 'All-embracing'.

Two nets to avoid in the Duat: in a pool (left) and stretched between two pegs (right).

---

**Self-Catering in the Duat**

In Spell 189, after repeatedly stating what he will eat in the Duat (mainly four loaves from the house of Horus and three from the house of Thoth in the Duat, and adamantly not faeces or urine) and specifically where ('under that sycamore of Hathor' or 'under the branches of the *djebat-nefret* tree'), the deceased is finally asked by the obscurely named One who Cannot Count, 'Will you live on someone else's goods everyday?' To which he replies that, in addition to the abovementioned divinely provided supplies, he ploughs the lands in the Field of Reeds, quickly refuting the demon's thinly veiled insinuation that he's an afterlife freeloader. These fields, the deceased relates, are guarded by the twin children of the King of Lower Egypt, and ploughed by 'the greatest of the gods of the sky and of the gods of the earth'.

---

## What to Eat and Drink

Certain spells will also ensure that you don't resort to eating faeces, drinking urine or walking with your head downwards whilst in the Duat. They can provide bread and other food that the gods live on. Bread of white emmer or the bread of Geb and beer of red barley of Hapi in the Pure Place comprise the preferred menu in the Duat, to be eaten under the branches of the tree of Hathor. The day barque and the night barque of the sun god also distribute bread and beer, though if all else fails the seven cows and their bull provide daily servings of bread and beer.

◄ PLACES OF INTEREST ►

Scanning the content of your Book of the Dead, you notice that the main features of the Duat are its gates, mounds and caverns, and so you set about trying to memorize their appearances and occupants. The Duat's geography is rather confusing to the newly

The Lake of Fire surrounded by baboons.

departed. Glancing at the first spell in the Book, you might become concerned about the snakes of Rostau, for example, who live on the flesh of men and gulp down their blood; luckily the spell helps to ward off such snakes. Regarding Rostau itself, you quickly learn that its southern gate is at Naref and its northern gate is in the Mound of Osiris. Spell 17 adds that there is a Lake of Fire between Naref and the House of the Entourage. The Lake of Fire burns sinners and purifies the righteous, and is a feature of Egyptian afterlife geography since the time of the Old Kingdom; its location, however, changes over time. In the New Kingdom, the Lake of Fire is typically depicted as a square or rectangular pool of water, with a baboon at each side, each accompanied by the hieroglyphic symbol for fire. In the Book of Two Ways, it can be accessed by two gates: the Gate of Darkness and the Gate of Fire.

## Gates of the Duat

Perhaps the most important feature of the Duat's landscape are its gates, because you must pass through them to reach Osiris. The Duat's landscape consists of a number of subdivisions, like a city divided into sectors, each only accessible through one gate – or like a palace or temple, in which the further one passes along its axis the more restricted access becomes.

The Duat's gates are sometimes depicted as quite elaborate, decorated with *ankh* and *djed* signs, and displaying *khekher* friezes (rows of upright bundled reeds, used to decorate the upper part of walls) and cavetto cornices (an outward curving feature at the top of walls). The number of gates differs depending on the spell; according to Spells 144 and 147 there are seven gates before Osiris is reached, each with a keeper, a guard and a reporter – all fearsome demons armed with knives, or the slightly less terrifying ears of corn. Some are mummiform and animal-headed, others are purely animals. Arriving at the first gate of the Duat, you are confronted by

Animal-headed guardians protect the gates of the Duat.

a keeper named 'He whose face is inverted, the many-shaped'. Beside him you spot the guard, called 'Eavesdropper', while the reporter is appropriately called 'Loud-voiced'. After you have looked up each demon's name in the Book of the Dead and spoken it aloud, the gatekeeper declares you worthy to pass, letting you through to the next division of the Duat and the further obstacles beyond. If any of the keepers look less than impressed with you, Spell 144 provides a long speech, aiming to convince them of your worthiness; it urges you to point out, among other things, that you were born in Rostau; that you lead the gods in the horizon in the entourage about Osiris; that you are a master of spirits; and that you carry the Eye of Horus. Afterwards, if this still doesn't work, you can follow the spell's suggestion that you tell the keeper that your name is mightier than his, and that you are one who 'raises up truth to Re and who destroys the might of Apophis': 'I am one who opens up the firmament,' you should say, 'who drives off the storm, who makes the crew of Re alive, and who raises up offerings to the place where they are.'

On the other hand, if you go by Spell 146, there are a lot more gates to get through: 21 in the 'House of Osiris in the Field of Reeds', each manned by two demons, a female guardian and a male door-keeper. The first you encounter is the 'Mistress of trembling; lofty of battlements; Chieftainess; Mistress of destruction; One who fore-tells matters, who repels storms and who rescues the robbed among those who come from afar' – rather a mouthful to pronounce when confronted by a terrifying (and armed) demonic creature! The doorkeeper, on the other hand, is succinctly called 'Terrible', which is a little easier to say under stress. Among the subsequent gate god-desses is the eighth guardian, called, 'Hot of flames, destructive of heat, sharp of blade, swift of hand, who kills without warning, whom none pass by for fear of her pain'. Her door-keeper is called 'He who protects himself' – not surprising given the violent nature of his gate goddess.

---

**Why So Many Different Numbers of Gates?**
In the Book of Dead we have met two different numbers of gates, either
7 or 21. To make the matter more confusing, in the Book of Gates, one
of the afterlife books carved into the walls of New Kingdom royal
tombs, there are 12 gates, one for each hour of the night, again each
guarded by a demon. These inconsistencies are a result of the ancient
Egyptians' unwillingness ever to discard an old idea – why remove
a potentially correct spell, when you can just cite all the alternatives?

---

## Mounds

Whilst wandering in the Duat, one of the features of the landscape
that might catch your attention are its numerous mounds. Of the
fourteen mounds mentioned in Spell 149, eleven are green and three
are yellow. The first mound is green. There, men live on *shen*-loaves
and jugs of beer. The god Re-Horakhety lives in the second mound
(which is also green). The third mound (green again) is more sinis-
ter: this is the mound of spirits, over which none travel, 'it contains
spirits, and its flame is efficient for burning'. The fourth mound is
(you guessed it) green and has very high twin mountains; it is 300
rods long and 150 rods wide. A 70-cubit-long snake, known as the
'Caster of Knives', lives there and decapitates and eats the heads of
spirits to survive. The fifth mound (green) is a Mound of Spirits,
which men do not pass, 'the spirits who are in it are 7 cubits from
their buttocks, and they live on in the shades of the inert ones'. The
sixth mound (green) is a 'cavern sacred to the gods, secret from
spirits and inaccessible to the dead' and appears to be inhabited
by an eel-like creature. The god who lives there is 'Feller of the
*adju*-fish'. If you climb this mound, you must visit the gods within,
prepare flat cakes for them and use your magic to stop the Feller of
*adju*-fish from having power over you.

The seventh mound (green) is the Mountain of the Rerek-Snake. This snake is 7 cubits long and lives on spirits. He is a formidable beast and you should fear his poison and bite; the Book usefully suggests that you invoke the violent god Mafdet (see p. 154) to cut off his head. A god called 'High One of Hahotep' lives in the eighth mound (green) and guards it so that none can come near. The ninth mound is yellow (surprise!), and called 'Ikesy-town and the Eye which captures'. This town is said to be 'hidden from the gods, of which the spirits are afraid to learn the name, from which none go in or out except that august god who is in his Egg (the creator god, probably Re-Atum), who puts fear of him into the gods and the dread of him into the spirits: it opens with fire, and its breath is destruction to noses and mouths'. The tenth mound is called 'Plateau' and is yellow. Despite its unassuming name, this is a frightening place, where you must command the inhabitants to lie on their bellies until you have passed, so that they cannot take your spirit or shade. The eleventh mound is green and full of secrets; these are so secret in fact that the spirits don't come or go from it for fear of revealing what they see. The twelfth mound (green) is known as 'Mound of Wenet, which is in front of Rostau'. The gods and spirits cannot come near this mound and four cobras dwell there, each called 'Destruction'. The thirteenth mound is green and called 'He who opens his mouth, a basin of water'. No one has power over this mound. Its water is fire, such that no one can drink from it, and its river is filled with papyrus. The (final!) fourteenth mound, called 'Mound of Kheraha', is yellow. It diverts the Nile and causes it to come laden with barley. The snake that belongs to it is in the cavern of Elephantine at the source of the Nile.

## Caverns

Travelling through the Duat, you also come across 12 caverns, each inhabited by multiple, surprisingly helpful deities. The gods of the eighth cavern are mysterious of shape and breathe air; of them, there

The caverns of the Duat and their inhabitants.

are those who follow Osiris, who grant that you be at rest in your mummy; as well as 'He who Stands up', who allows you to worship Re when he rises; and 'He who is hidden, who makes you strong in the hall of Geb', among many others – Sherem, for example, stops evil from coming close to you in the Duat. The gods of the tenth cavern are said to cry aloud and possess holy mysteries. Here, those who belong to the sunshine give you light. In the other caverns, the god Iqeh grants that you be in the presence of Re, and that you cross the sky for ever with him; Iqen drives away all evil; the Destroyer clears your vision, so that you may see the sunshine-god; and 'She whose head is red' ensures that you have power over the waters.

◀ GETTING AROUND ▶

The Book of the Dead includes little mention of how you traverse the Duat; it seems that you are meant to undertake your journey on foot or by boat on the river. Nevertheless, if you ever become tired of walking or suffer from seasickness you can magically transform into a variety of forms: Spell 13 allows you to become a falcon or a phoenix; Spell 77 transforms you into a falcon of gold, 4 cubits long and with wings formed of a green stone; Spell 79 allows you to become an elder of the tribunal; Spells 81A and B let you turn into a lotus; Spell 83 transforms you into a phoenix; Spell 84, a heron; Spell 85, into a living soul, who will not enter the place of execution; Spell 86, a swallow; Spell 87, a snake; and Spell 88, a crocodile. You might even take the form of gods, such as Atum or Ptah. Finally, just to cover all bases, Spell 76 allows you to transform into whatever shape you desire.

At various points in your journey, however, the celestial ferryman complicates your travel plans. When meeting him (his name is Mahaf), the Book says that you must ask him to go and wake up Aqen, who is in charge of the ferry. But before he leaves to awaken Aqen, Mahaf starts making excuses as to why the boat isn't riverworthy. Ask him to bring the 'built-up boat of Khnum from the Lake of Feet' and Mahaf will tell you that it's in pieces and stored in the dockyard. When Mahaf points out that, 'she has no planks, she has no end-pieces, she has no rubbing-pieces, she has no oar-loops,' you must remember to remind him, 'Her planks are the drops of moisture which are on the lips of Babi; her end-pieces are the hair which is under the tail of Seth; her rubbing-pieces are the sweat which is on the ribs of Babi; her oar-loops are the hands of the female counterpart of Horus. She is built by the Eye of Horus who shall steer her for me.'

According to the Book, Mahaf will then become worried about who will guard his boat, to which you should suggest the (unidentified) *senemty*-animal. Later, Mahaf argues that the weather is windy and the boat has no mast. You should respond by telling him to bring the phallus of Babi, as that will do the job admirably. After some time, Mahaf will relent and leave to fetch Aqen ('What is it?' Aqen will say. 'I was asleep.'). Aqen, far from being your sensible saviour, introduces his own problems, one being the lack of a bailer, leaving you to suggest a solution as usual. Even when the boat finally arrives, your problems aren't over yet – before you can go sailing, each component of the boat demands to be named.

◀ THE LOCALS (OR THE DENIZENS OF THE DUAT) ▶

In death, not only do you have to contend with the unfamiliar geography of the Duat and deal with strange gate demons, but the general population around you are also a rather fearsome bunch. As you walk along the pathways, your way through the darkness lit by magic, you might encounter creatures walking with backwards heads, their eyes in their knees, who are demons known for severing heads. Rebellious enemies are also a source of danger, so in addition to your garment, sandals, staff and loin-cloth, the Book of the Dead urges you to bring all your weapons to sever their necks. Basically, any creature you meet could potentially be hostile, but as long as you know the demon's name, you gain control over him, turning him from a threat into a protector. In this manner, gods with names like 'He who burns up the rebellious', 'He who takes hearts for food', 'He who dances in blood' and 'He who hacks up human dead' become a little less intimidating.

Demon animals also interfere and have to be fought off with the power of spells backed up with the threat of a large knife or spear. Crocodiles in particular might rob you of your magical abilities, so if you ever become surrounded by a group of eight crocodiles led by the one who lives on the Unwearying Stars, you should fight them off with your spear. As usual, when faced with a threat, knowing the name of your enemy is an advantage. 'Get back! Retreat! Get back, you dangerous one!' Spell 31 relates about an encounter with a crocodile, 'Do not come against me, do not live by my magic; may I not have to tell this name of yours to the Great God who sent you; 'Messenger' is the name of one and Bedty is the name of the other.'

There are also evil snakes, including the *rerek*-snake, to whom you say, 'O rerek-snake, take yourself off, for Geb protects me; get up, for you have eaten a mouse, which Re detests, and you have chewed the bones of a putrid cat.' One snake bites an ass and is referred to as 'He who swallowed an ass'. At other times, you must

---

**The God Babi**

Referred to as 'with red ear and purple anus', Babi was an aggressive baboon, who lived on human entrails and even stole offerings from the obscurely named 'goddess of the sedan chair'. He is sometimes associated with Seth and could use his powers to ward off snakes and other dangerous creatures. His phallus served as the door bolt of the sky, allowing it to be opened and closed, and also as the mast of the ferryboat of the Duat. Though he lacks a formal cult, Babi's phallic associations, along with his divine virility, led him to be invoked in spells for the protection and healing of the penis. We have already met Babi as 'eldest son of Osiris' in Chapter 3 and as the god that deeply offended the Universal Lord in *The Contendings of Horus and Seth,* retold in Chapter 4.

---

fight Apophis, assuming the identity of Re to do so. You might also get pestered by the *apshai*-beetle during your journey, but the spell to repel him is 'Begone from me, O Crooked-lips! I am Khnum, Lord of Peshnu, who dispatches the words of the gods to Re, and I report affairs to their master.'

There are also afterlife demons that try to tempt you away from your *maat*-like behaviour, rather than just outright trying to kill you (again). One such being to look out for is the butler of the hostile dead, Gebga, normally described as being a black raven. He lives on excrement and tempts you to eat excrement too by explaining that it is the excrement of Horus and Seth (and so presumably not *that* awful). This temptation is a common theme. At one point in the Coffin Texts, the deceased is tempted to eat faeces from the buttocks of Osiris. This reflects an upside-down world – a common aspect of the Duat – but one that you must reject.

You might also come across the demon Iaau – a manifestation of the living world reversed. He lives on faeces, drinks urine, has a tongue between his legs and a phallus in his mouth. Iaau is said

The Duat is not a place to enter unarmed. Here Nakht fights the pesky *apshai*-beetle with a knife, three crocodiles and later a snake called 'him who swallowed an ass'.

to have been in the belly of the creator before existence came into being. He was eventually expelled like excrement and became the incarnation of the negative.

---

**Shezmu**

Shezmu was a deity to befriend rather than to make an enemy of. As god of wine and oil presses, you might expect that he'd be a jovial presence in the Duat, and perhaps he is, but he also puts his presses to more bloody uses, squeezing the heads of the damned for one. He also butchers and cooks gods so that the king can eat their bodies and absorb their strength. On the other hand, he does supply the gods with perfume.

---

## ◄ 8 ►

## YOUR JUDGMENT
## AND LIFE AS AN AKH

Having navigated your way through the trials of the Duat, you now reach your ultimate destination – the Judgment Hall of Osiris, called the Hall of the Double Justice. After being questioned, and after each part of the hall's gateway has demanded that you speak its name (for example, the door-posts will halt you saying 'We will not let you enter by us unless you tell our name' but you can answer: '"Plummet of Thoth" is your name'), the doorway asks to which god you should be announced.

'Tell it to the Interpreter of the Two Lands', you should reply.
'Who is the Interpreter of the Two Lands?'
'It is Thoth.'
Perhaps overhearing his name, Thoth now approaches to question you further.
'Now,' says Thoth, 'why have you come?'
'I have come here to report', you reply.
'What is your condition?'
'I am free of all wrongdoing, I avoided the strife of those in their day, I am not one of them.'
'To whom shall I announce you?'
'To him whose roof is of fire, whose walls are living cobras, the floor of whose house is in the flood.'
'Who is he?'
'He is Osiris.'
'Proceed, you are announced, the Eye is your bread, the Eye is your beer, the Eye is your offering on earth.'

◀ THE JUDGMENT OF OSIRIS AND THE COUNCIL OF 42 ▶

*Every god you served on earth, you [now] see face to face.*
HARPER'S SONG FROM THE TOMB OF NEFERHOTEP

Judgment time. Clad in white garments and sandals, anointed with myrrh and adorned with black eye-paint, you are escorted into the Hall of the Double Justice by Anubis and quickly realize that it is arranged like a chapel: its roof is supported by columns, its upper walls decorated with *maat*-feathers and rearing, live cobras. Forty-two knife-wielding mummiform gods crouch in lines at either side of the hall, human, crocodile, snake and lion faces staring intently ahead, each wearing a *maat*-feather atop a wig, while at the hall's centre, further deities, more illustrious, formally observe your arrival. Instantly recognizable thanks to his ibis head, Thoth stands closest to you, scribal palette in hand, ready to record the results of your trial. Beyond, Osiris, green-skinned and wrapped in linen, gripping his crook and flail, sits enthroned beneath a canopy approached by steps, silently watching proceedings. His sisters Isis and Nephthys stand behind him. To be in the presence of such powerful forces alone might be enough to rattle the nerves, but it is the fearsome creature Ammit that causes your hands and legs

Osiris (far left) oversees the weighing of the heart of the deceased (praising, far right).

Ammit (right) waits patiently for Thoth to record the fate of the deceased.

to tremble. This beast, with the head of a crocodile, the torso of a leopard/lion and the hindparts of a hippopotamus – each a formidable creature on its own – crouches beside a set of scales, ready to devour you if your sinful acts in life outweigh the feather of *maat*. Her mouth is gaping, her teeth bared. She looks hungry.

Osiris glaring on, you first declare your innocence to him as Lord of Truth, stating, among other things, that you have not done falsehood against men, not deprived an orphan of his property, not done what the gods detest and have not killed or commanded to kill. Arms raised in adoration, you next approach each of the 42 assessor gods in turn, those 'who live on those who cherish evil and who gulp down their blood', announcing the name of each one and stating a particular sin that you did not commit. 'O Far-strider who came forth from Heliopolis, I have done no falsehood,' you say to the first god in the line. 'O Fire-embracer who came forth from Kheraha, I have not robbed,' you say to the next. And so on. To Nosey from Hermopolis, you have not been rapacious; to Fiery Eyes from Letopolis, you have done no crookedness; to Bone-breaker from Herakleopolis, you have not told lies; to the Eater of entrails from the House of Thirty, you have not committed perjury. Among the 42 transgressions are babbling, being sullen, stealing

The human-faced heart scarab of Sebekemsaf.

bread, misbehaving, eavesdropping, being impatient and being loud-voiced, alongside the more serious-sounding killing a sacred bull, blaspheming in your city and conjuring magic against the king. Finally, just to be absolutely clear on the matter, you declare your innocence a further time, this time addressing all the gods in the hall, and cheerfully – perhaps over-cheerfully – reminding them that you 'gulp down truth'.

Once you have appeased the 42 gods, it is time to stand before Osiris again. Anubis sets up the scales and Thoth, now in baboon form, squats on top of the pole at their centre (or perhaps beside them). Painlessly, your heart leaves your body and gently floats over to the left-hand scale pan. For some, this might be the time to start worrying, but luckily for you, your mummy was well prepared for this eventuality. Spell 30, inscribed on a heart scarab, placed above your true heart within the mummy wrappings, magically forces it to hide all your wrongdoing, leaving an unblemished record to be recited before Osiris. 'Do not stand up as a witness against me,' the spell reads, addressing the heart, 'do not be opposed to me in the tribunal, do not be hostile to me in the presence of the Keeper of the Balance...' And so, with a confident smile, you watch your heart balance against the feather of *maat*; your afterlife is assured. Thoth, now human-bodied and ibis-headed again, jots down the results on his papyrus scroll, and turns to address the Great Ennead, announcing that he has judged your heart and your deeds have been found to be righteous. In particular, he notes that you haven't taken offerings from the temples or told lies when alive. The Ennead, convinced, accepts the judgment and Horus brings you once more before Osiris, telling him that your heart has been shown to be true, without a sin committed against any deity. Thoth has recorded the judgment, the Ennead has been told and the goddess Maat has witnessed events. Bread and beer should be awarded you, so you can spend eternity like a follower of Horus.

Now comes your turn to speak directly to the gods.

*Here I am in your presence, O Lord of the West. There is no wrong-doing in my body, I have not wittingly told lies, there has been no second fault. Grant that I may be like the favoured ones who are in your suite, O Osiris, one greatly favoured by the good god, one loved of the Lord of the Two Lands...*
BOOK OF THE DEAD, SPELL 30B

The gods now announce you as 'true of voice', a follower of Osiris and also, rather kindly, give back your heart. The god Atum, physical creation itself, ties a wreath of flowers around your head and then, finally, exhausted yet jubilant, you are free to go on your way, leaving through a door at the far end of the hall, opposite the one through which you entered.

◄ BEING *AKH* – A TRANSFIGURED SPIRIT ►

Successful before the tribunal, you exit the Hall of Judgment as a member of the blessed dead. Your *ba* and *ka* spirits have been reunited and you have been declared an *akh* (see box p. 196). Reserved only for those who pass the judgment test, not all of the dead hold the status of *akh*; those who failed to find their way through the Duat – who failed to combine their *ba* and *ka* and thus remain eternally non-transfigured – are classified as *mut*, 'dead', while those judged unworthy receive a second death, obliterated from existence via the sharp teeth and bowels of Ammit, or after a period of torture in the Duat at the hands of the 'slayers of Osiris … sharp of fingers' in the 'slaughter place' of the god.

### Akhu and Enemies

The aim of every Egyptian was to become an *akh,* rather than 'an enemy'.

The word *akh* (plural *akhu*) is difficult to translate; it seems not to designate a new evolution of being, but rather a status conferred upon the deceased. Regarded as a person that has become one with the light, an *akh* existed in a glorified state, effective and transfigured, and free to travel and dwell anywhere it wished, whether that be with the gods in the sky or the Duat, or among the living on earth.

Enemies of order, a class of people rather than those judged unworthy of a blessed state, existed at all times as representatives of chaos. These enemies received constant punishment, rather than a second death, being forced to eat their own excrement or walk upside down. The gods drank their blood, and their flesh was cooked. Placing enemies in cauldrons appears to have been a typical punishment in the Duat; in the Book of Caverns, three sets of cauldrons are depicted, each held aloft by arms emerging from the ground, called the 'arms of the Place of Annihilation'. The first cauldron contained the heads and hearts of enemies; the second, the upside-down decapitated and bound enemies themselves; and the third, the flesh, *ba*-souls and shadows of the enemies of Re and Osiris.

Two cauldrons: headless bodies are cooked on the left, hearts and heads on the right.

Nefertari plays the game *Senet*, symbolically defeating death, her invisible opponent.

### ◄ NOW WHAT? ►

So you've passed Osiris' judgment, appeased the 42 gods of the divine tribunal, and officially been declared an *akh*, 'now what?' you might ask. Being free to move throughout the created world unhindered, many options present themselves, not necessarily mutually exclusive. For one, you could spend your afterlife travelling with the sun god, navigating his boat through the sky and fighting off any aggressors for him, whilst also making offerings and mixing with the unwearying stars. You could enter the presence of the Ennead and become like one of them, or have a quiet drink beside the Lake of Two Knives before setting off to watch the sacred *bulti* fish in the stream of turquoise, as well as the *abdju* fish. You also get the opportunity to see Horus holding the standards of Thoth and Maat.

As an *akh*, you can decide to spend some time in the Kingdom of Osiris, too, dining at his table in the 'Beautiful West'. You could also leave the Duat in the morning and spend your time close to your tomb, playing draughts perhaps, only to return to the Duat in the evening to rest. You also have the option of joining the tribunal of gods that judge between Horus and Seth. There is never an indication in the Book of the Dead, however, that you are able to spend time with other spirits, not even your family and friends (though you could visit your parents in the Field of Reeds, see below). Your only companions in the Duat are the gods, whose characteristics you have assumed in death.

Living among the gods, you now appear as a divinity: your upper torso is formed from lapis lazuli, your hair is jet black and scattered with lapis lazuli. Your face shines like Re because it is covered in gold, inlaid with lapis lazuli. You will also wear a vestment of fine linen and be adorned with gold. In death, the individual parts of your body also become imbued with divinity and are associated with various gods. You become Osiris and Re, and act as a source of light, rising eternally.

◀ THE FIELD OF REEDS AND THE FIELD OF OFFERINGS ▶

Perhaps the most familiar place that you could visit in death was the Field of Reeds, described and illustrated in some detail in Spells 109 and 110 of the Book of the Dead. A part of this is reserved for you. Passing through the great walls of iron, which block access to the unworthy, you reach the Field of Reeds by boat, part of a flotilla that includes the sun god's own solar barque. After disembarking, you spot the two great trees of turquoise, from between which the sun rises each day, and go to pay your respects to the Great Ennead of the gods, feeling privileged to meet them in person. You then sail along the river towards your agricultural fields, passing mounds and waterways, including 'the waterway of the white hippopotamus'. Your Book of the Dead informs you that this location is 'a thousand leagues in length; its breadth has not been told. There are no fish in it; there are not any snakes in it.' As you float along the river, you also notice the waterway known as 'The Horns of the Mistress of Purification', which is a thousand leagues in length and breadth.

Activities in the Field of Reeds.

After some time, you reach your plot of land. Not wanting to perform any actual labour yourself, however, you use your magic to summon your *shabtis*, workers who perform any and all agricultural tasks for you; *shabti* statues placed in the tomb should

*Shabtis* performed tasks in the Duat for the deceased.

be inscribed with Spell 6 of the Book of the Dead to ensure their loyalty and labour in the afterlife. Thanks to their hard work, planting seeds, ploughing and harvesting in the presence of the 'souls of the easterners', the barley grows to be 5 cubits tall, and the emmer to be 7 cubits. You notice yourself that in this supernatural space, a place that encourages growth, you now stand 9 cubits in height. Here, there is an abundance of all good things, but none of the creatures that pestered you in life. You can plough, reap, eat, drink and copulate, just as you did on earth, although it's best not to shout – apparently this is banned. Having watched your *shabtis* tend to the fields, you next stop by the heron of plenty, who supplies you with all manner of provisions, including food and drink. On the move again, you sail past further mounds and cities, many with unusual names, such as the Town of the Great Goddess, the swamp-land, the Town of Fair Offerings, Provision Town, the Town of the Milk Goddess and Town of Union, before reaching Qenqenet, where you pay your respects to your parents. Your final destination is again the Great Ennead, who can never receive too much praise.

---

**But Where Was the Field of Reeds?**

As with many aspects of Egyptian afterlife beliefs, ideas changed over the thousands of years of history. At first, the Field of Reeds existed south of the Winding Waterway, that is, south of the ecliptic in the sky, and served as the place of purification before the deceased entered the sky. Its counterpart was the Field of Offerings, located north of the ecliptic; it is this place that the deceased actually longed to visit, rowing there in a boat. By the New Kingdom, the Field of Reeds had taken on the characteristics of the Field of Offerings, and was now regarded as existing somewhere beyond the eastern horizon. Book of the Dead Spell 110 even relates that the Field of Reeds was within the Field of Offerings, highlighting just how entangled the two, previously separate, locations had become by the New Kingdom.

---

◄ STORIES OF THE DUAT ►

## Setna's Descent into the Duat

Although, strictly speaking, you had to be a deity or deceased to enter the Duat, those powerful of magic could bend the rules of nature. One such individual was Si-Osire, son of Setna and Meheweskhe, whose adventures are preserved on Papyrus BM 604, copied during the 1st century AD. One day, while Setna was at home in Memphis, purifying himself in preparation for a festival, he heard wailing outside. Looking out from his window, he saw the coffin of a rich man being carried through the streets towards the necropolis. Then, looking downward, he saw the body of a poor man, wrapped in a mat, being carried out of the city; there was total silence and no one walked behind him. Setna turned to Si-Osire and exclaimed how much happier the rich man must be, thanks to his wonderful funerary procession, than the poor man who has nothing. Unexpectedly, however, Si-Osire replied that he hoped that Setna would receive the same fate in the West as the poor man. Setna was understandably shocked and saddened that his own son would hope for such a terrible destiny for him. But then Si-Osire said a curious thing, asking his father if he wished to see the fate of both the poor man and the rich man in the West. Setna was astonished: 'How can you do this?' he asked, but, as he spoke, he became disorientated and had no idea where he was.

When Setna regained his bearings, he was standing in the fourth hall of the Duat. All around him, people were plaiting ropes, which in turn were gnawed by donkeys. Provisions of water and bread were suspended above other people, but as they jumped to grab them, men dug pits beneath their feet. Leaving these men to their torment, Setna and Si-Osire then entered the fifth hall, where noble spirits stood in their ranks. Those accused of violence were pleading in a doorway beyond, its pivot fixed in the right eye of a man who was himself howling in pain. Setna and Si-Osire next passed into the sixth hall, where the gods of the council of the inhabitants of the West stood in their ranks and the servants of the West stood giving reports.

In the seventh hall, Setna witnessed the secret form of Osiris, seated upon a throne of fine gold and wearing the *atef*-crown. Anubis stood to his left and Thoth to his right, while the gods of the council of inhabitants flanked them. The feather of *maat* rested on its scale at the centre of the room, measuring people's faults against their good deeds. Thoth observed and wrote down the results, while Anubis passed on information to him. Those whose bad deeds outweighed their good were eaten by Ammit, and their *ba*-spirits and corpses destroyed; such individuals would never breathe again. Conversely, those found to have lived good lives were brought among the council of the Lord of the West, and their *ba*-spirits ascended to the sky with the noble spirits. Those whose good and bad deeds balanced joined the excellent spirits serving Sokar-Osiris.

As they scanned the hall, taking in the sights and sounds around them, Setna spotted a man wrapped in royal linen standing beside

Osiris; he was clearly of very high rank. Setna stepped forward to take a closer look.

'Don't you see,' Si-Osire said to his father, 'this rich man who is wrapped in a garment of royal linen and who is near the place where Osiris is? He is that poor man whom you saw as they were bringing him out from Memphis with no one walking behind him and who was wrapped in a mat.' After death, Si-Osire went on to explain, the poor man was brought to the Duat, where he was judged by the gods. They found his good deeds more numerous than his bad, and so transferred the rich man's funerary equipment to him. As a noble spirit, he now served Sokar-Osiris, and was allowed to stand close to Osiris.

The wealthy man was also brought to the Duat, Si-Osire said, but his faults were more numerous than his good deeds. It was commanded that he be punished in the West, and so his right eye became the pivot of the door of the West, his mouth eternally locked open in tortured howls of pain. This is why Si-Osire hoped that his father's eventual fate in the West would match the poor man's. Eager to learn more, Setna asked his son about the other people he had seen in the halls of the Duat. Those plaiting ropes being gnawed by donkeys are the counterparts of those on earth who are cursed by god, Si-Osire replied; they work day and night for their livelihood, but their women rob them behind their backs, so they find no bread to eat. Whatever happened to them on earth, happens to them in the West. Those whose water and bread were suspended above them, always out of reach, they are the counterpart of the people on earth whose lives are before them, but god digs a pit under their feet to stop them from discovering it.

'Take it to heart, my father Setna,' Si-Osire said, 'that the one who is beneficent on earth, they are beneficent to him in the West, while the one who is evil, they are evil to him. This is established [and will not be changed] ever.' As Si-Osire finished speaking, he and his father emerged, hand in hand, into the necropolis of Memphis.

## Meryre's Journey into the Duat

Though ghosts (and Si-Osire) seem to have had no trouble dividing their time between the land of the living and the Duat, leaving the Duat is immensely difficult, if not impossible, for most humans. One account concerning this is found in the *Tale of Meryre*, set in the reign of King Sisobek and preserved on Papyrus Vandier, dated to the late 6th century BC. Meryre is a skilled magician and scribe, so skilled in fact that the magicians of Pharaoh's court keep his existence a secret from the king for fear that they might all lose their jobs. One night, however, Pharaoh falls ill; his food tastes like clay and his beer like water. He is covered in sweat. Summoned to his presence, his magicians exclaim in horror when they see him, and are reminded of an occasion in the past, when King Djedkare suffered from the same problem. Scouring their books for any information, they soon discover that Sisobek has only seven days left to live, and realize that the only person capable of extending his life is Meryre. For the first time, the jealous magicians are forced to reveal his existence to the king, but they realize that this provides the perfect opportunity to be rid of Meryre forever.

Meryre is duly summoned to court and Pharaoh asks how his life might be prolonged. No doubt taking his king by surprise, Meryre begins to cry, explaining through his tears that in order to extend Pharaoh's life, he, Meryre, will have to offer his own: whatever happens, someone will have to die. Reluctant to offer himself to the gods as Sisobek's substitute, Meryre takes some convincing before agreeing to save his king. Indeed, Pharaoh has to promise him posthumous honours and commit to keeping his name alive in the temples, before he agrees. Meryre also asks for certain favours in return for his sacrifice. He makes Pharaoh swear in front of Ptah that his wife will be cared for and that he won't allow any man to look at her or enter his home. More menacingly, he asks that the children of the jealous magicians, who without a doubt informed Pharaoh of his existence in the sure knowledge that it would mean his death, be killed. Pharaoh agrees to both requests. Satisfied, Meryre returns home to shave and don a fine linen robe in preparation for his quest into the afterlife. Meanwhile, Pharaoh travels to Heliopolis, to offer to the gods, thereby securing Meryre a safe journey.

A long break in the text follows.

As the story resumes, Meryre is explaining to Pharaoh that he will approach Osiris and present prayers in his name; clearly, the time has come for Meryre to leave. He tells Pharaoh to stay far from him – not even to look – and without further ado steps into the Duat. Within moments of his arrival, before he can even orient himself, Meryre is approached by the goddess Hathor, who greets him warmly and asks him what he wants. 'To ask for a prolongation of life for pharaoh,' he responds, so she takes him to Osiris. Skipping all pleasantries, the Great God questions Meryre about the condition of Egypt's temples, among other things, and only when satisfied that all is well among the living does he grant Pharaoh an extension to his life. At the same time, however, he denies Meryre the right to return to the living, confining him to the Duat for all eternity.

Though Meryre is stuck in the Duat, Hathor, of course, is not limited by such restrictions, and goes to visit the living to celebrate one of her festivals. Upon her return, Meryre eagerly asks her about everything she had seen – has Pharaoh kept his promises? Unfortunately, it is not good news: Pharaoh has made Meryre's wife his own Great Royal Wife, taken possession of his house and killed his son. Taken aback, Meryre bursts into tears and asks how Pharaoh had come to behave in such a despicable manner. Her response cannot have come as a surprise – the jealous magicians had encouraged his acts, manipulating the weak-minded king with their trickery. Filled with anger and thoughts of revenge, Meryre takes a lump of clay and moulds it into the shape of a man. Using his magic, he animates the figure and commands him to do all that he says, before despatching him to the world of the living to confront Pharaoh.

Upon arriving at court, the clay man enters Pharaoh's presence and demands that his magicians be burned in the furnace of Mut. Sisobek is shocked and sits motionless, frozen. After some time – perhaps contemplating his nefarious actions – he summons his magicians, but none know what to say or do. While they debate, the clay man repeats his demand again and again – a rather intimidating distraction. In the end, faced with the demands of a supernatural being (and perhaps safe in the knowledge that he can always find new magicians), Pharaoh decides to do as instructed and sends his magicians to be executed. Victorious, carrying a bouquet of flowers, the clay man returns to the Duat to tell Meryre of all that had occurred. The ecstatic Meryre celebrates and takes his flowers to Osiris, who is confused. 'Have you been to earth?' the god asks, and so Meryre explains about his magical clay man.

Sadly, the rest of the tale is lost.

◄ EVEN GODS DIE ►

Though obsessed with permanence, the Egyptians did envision an end to all things, even the gods. The authority of a god was not only limited by location or responsibility, it was also limited by time. Like every living being in creation, the gods had a fixed lifespan. Existence, however, was regarded as cyclical. The sun god might die each day, but in the middle of the night he was re-energized, ready to be reborn in the morning. Death was a stage in the process of rejuvenation, as it was only through death that a person grown weak and old could be reinvigorated with youth.

This diversity is a key element of creation, it is what separates it from the infinite, inert, undifferentiated Nun. To the Egyptians everything that existed could be named and was unique, separate, active and diverse. To be otherwise would be non-existent, inactive, undifferentiated. The gods, then, as part of this world, had to be

At the end of time, the world will return to the waters of Nun.

diverse, had to be unique and had to be limited. Death is the ultimate limitation. They may be powerful beings, but the gods have to play by the same rules as everyone else in order to remain in existence.

◄ IT'S THE END OF THE WORLD AS WE KNOW IT ►
(BUT YOU SHOULD FEEL FINE)

*I am going to destroy all I have made, and this world is going to return to the Water [Nun] and the Flood, like its first state.*
BOOK OF THE DEAD, SPELL 175

At the end of time, millions of years from now, the Egyptians envisioned the waters of Nun reclaiming the created world, an act of destruction initiated by Atum himself, to bring it back to its original

The Nile flood at Giza.

state. Only Atum and Osiris would remain after this cataclysm, transformed into serpents without men knowing or gods seeing. In this time, they would sit in one place and mounds would be towns and towns would be mounds. It was not all bleak though. Still existent in the inert waters of Nun, Atum embodied all of physical creation, and Osiris the force of regeneration.

Like a great cliffhanger ending, at the end of time the potential for new life would remain.

## THE MYTH OF ANCIENT EGYPT

*A time will come when it will appear that the Egyptians*
*paid respect to divinity with faithful mind and painstaking*
*reverence – to no purpose. All their holy worship will be*
*disappointed and perish without effect, for divinity will*
*return from earth to heaven, and Egypt will be abandoned ...*
*O Egypt, Egypt, of your reverent deeds only stories will survive,*
*and they will be incredible to your children! Only words*
*cut in stone will survive to tell your faithful works...*
ASCLEPIUS, CHAPTER 24

The above quotation, part of a longer lament written by a Greek in Egypt under the Romans of the 2nd or 3rd centuries AD, illustrates that the Egyptians under later rule were acutely aware that the time of their gods was ending. Romans, such as the poet Juvenal, even treated the ancient religion with sarcastic contempt: 'Who does not know what monsters lunatic Egypt chooses to cherish?' he wrote, 'One part goes in for crocodile worship; one bows down to the ibis that feeds upon serpents; elsewhere a golden effigy shines, of a long-tailed holy monkey!' Shortly afterwards, the Egyptian gods did indeed retire from their land and many of their statues were burnt and destroyed as the population converted first to Christianity and then to Islam. All the while, the monuments of ancient Egypt slowly crumbled, the gods' images were attacked and occasionally their temples were adapted for new purposes. Words cut in stone remained, but their meaning was lost.

Over time, the ancient Egyptians themselves became mythic. Removed from the mundane reality of their everyday existence by time and imagination, the ancient Egyptians and their world, or

Over time, Egypt's monuments gradually vanished beneath the sands.

at least our fragmented understanding of it, has been adopted by people across the planet and retrofitted to serve whatever purpose exists in the imaginer's mind. The concept of ancient Egypt reflects a wonderland where anything is possible: from Biblical accounts of the Nile turning to blood, to hidden chambers of secrets beneath the paws of the Sphinx, Egypt is disconnected from history as a series of yesterdays and is instead a world of its own, separated from the physics and limitations of today. Portrayed as the inheritors of the lost wisdom of Atlantis, the builders of pyramid power plants, and as possessors of alien technology, the ancient Egyptians apparently had it all, yet the best evidence reveals a far simpler picture: a long-lived agricultural society, exploited by a tiny elite and a semi-divine monarchy, who developed a unique outlook and view, achieved highs and lows like any civilization and eventually (like all creations) transformed, entering new phases of existence.

The pharaohs are iconic, the monuments everlasting, but Tutankhamun and the Great Pyramid are not ancient Egypt, they are just tiny fragments of the whole. Alternative writers seem to believe otherwise; in their creations, the Great Pyramid plays a peculiarly central role in Egyptian civilization, as if the entire ancient world revolved around its once gleaming peak. Yet ignoring the fancies of new-agers and alternative theorists, even among scholars ancient Egypt itself remains mythic to some degree. Though new data appears all the time, evidence for lives and events so distant from our own time will, regrettably, forever remain incomplete; it will always be necessary to interpret ancient Egyptian civilization, especially given the idealized nature of most of the evidence, and where there is interpretation, there is imagination, no matter how hard we strive to shut it out.

Like chasing distant entities disappearing into the sunset, we map the Egyptians and chart their lives based on their shadows, measuring their footprints in the sand. Their true selves may remain elusive, just out of reach, but the force of their personalities is imprinted on discarded personal possessions, glimpsed among their glorious ruins, and, indeed, manifest in their myths.

An agricultural society: picking grapes for wine and preparing birds for dinner.

The Great Sphinx and pyramids of Giza: iconic symbols of Egypt.

From these scattered fragments, we each create our own simulation of ancient Egypt, some more accurate than others, some more fantastical, all incomplete, all unique. The myth of ancient Egypt is ever-changing, ever-renewing.

The ancient Egyptians themselves were obsessed with their names and deeds enduring, since if your name remained unspoken you would suffer a second, final, death. I like to imagine they'd be bemused by all the attention they receive, but see it as a sign of a job well done. So long as their names continued to be mentioned, would they care if modern people believe that the Great Pyramid was built with the help of Atlantean technology or aliens? Perhaps they might be offended that modern people want to remove them from their own awesome achievements, but so long as they are remembered, the main aim is achieved. Our modern myths of ancient Egypt serve their purposes remarkably well; they allow the Egyptians to reach out across time to us, filtered by the journey, re-jigged, but still containing traces of their identity. Like their gods, the ancient Egyptians are invisible, formless and can today only be experienced through their images.

They live on as myth.

Abbreviations used:
*JARCE* = *Journal of the American Research Center in Egypt*
*JEA* = *Journal of Egyptian Archaeology*

### General Egyptian Mythology and Religion

David, R., *Religion and Magic in Ancient Egypt* (London and New York, 2002).

Dunand, F., and C. M. Zivie-Coche, *Gods and Men in Egypt: 3000 BCE to 395 CE* (transl. D. Lorton; Ithaca, NY, and London, 2004).

Hart, G., *Egyptian Myths* (London and Austin, 1990).

Hornung, E., *Conceptions of God in Ancient Egypt: The One and the Many* (transl. J. Baines; Ithaca, NY, 1982).

Meeks, D., and C. Favard-Meeks, *Daily Life of the Egyptian Gods* (transl. G. M. Goshgarian; London and Ithaca, NY, 1997).

Morenz, S., *Egyptian Religion* (Ithaca, 1973).

Pinch, G., *Handbook of Egyptian Mythology* (Santa Barbara, Denver, Oxford, 2002).

—, *Egyptian Mythology: A Guide to the Gods, Goddesses and Traditions of Ancient Egypt* (Oxford and Santa Barbara, 2002).

—, *Egyptian Mythology: A Very Short Introduction* (Oxford and New York, 2004).

Quirke, S., *Ancient Egyptian Religion* (London and New York, 2000).

Redford, D., (ed.), *The Oxford Encyclopedia of Ancient Egypt* (3 vols; Oxford and New York, 2001).

—, (ed.), *The Oxford Essential Guide to Egyptian Mythology* (Oxford, 2003).

Shafer, B. E., (ed.), *Religion in Ancient Egypt: Gods, Myths, and Personal Practice* (London and Ithaca, NY, 1991).

Shaw, I., and P. Nicholson, *The BM Dictionary of Ancient Egypt* (London, 1995).

Spence, L., *Ancient Egyptian Myths and Legends* (1915).

Thomas, A., *Egyptian Gods and Myths* (Aylesbury, 1986).

Tyldesley, J., *Myths and Legends of Ancient Egypt* (London, 2010).

Wilkinson, R. H., *The Complete Gods and Goddesses of Ancient Egypt* (London and New York, 2003).

### Translations and Sources

Allen, J. P., *The Ancient Egyptian Pyramid Texts* (Leiden and Boston, 2005).

Bakir, A. el-M., *The Cairo Calendar No. 86637* (Cairo, 1966).

Betz, H. D., *The Greek Magical Papyri in Translation Including the Demotic Spells* (Chicago and London, 1986).

Borghouts, J. F., *Ancient Egyptian Magical Texts* (Leiden, 1978).

Diodorus Siculus, *Library of History* (transl. C. H. Oldfather; Book I; London and New York, 1933).

Faulkner, R., O., *The Ancient Egyptian Coffin Texts* (3 vols; Warminster, 1972–78).

—, *The Ancient Egyptian Book of the Dead* (ed. C. Andrews; London and New York, 1985).

Lichtheim, M., *Ancient Egyptian Literature* (3 vols; Berkeley and London, 1975–80).

Manetho, *Aegyptiaca* (transl. W. G. Wadell; London, 1940).

Meeks, D., *Mythes et légendes du Delta d'après le papyrus Brooklyn 47.218.84* (Cairo, 2006).

Parkinson, R., *Voices from Ancient Egypt: An Anthology of Middle Kingdom Writings* (London and Norman, 1991).

Plutarch, *Moralia*. Vol. V: *Isis and Osiris* (transl. F. C. Babbitt; London and Cambridge, MA, 1936).

Simpson, W. K., *et al.*, *The Literature of Ancient Egypt* (Cairo, 2003).

Smith, M., *Traversing Eternity: Texts for the Afterlife from Ptolemaic and Roman Egypt* (Oxford, 2009).

Vandier, J., *Le Papyrus Jumilhac* (Paris, 1961).

### Introduction

Baines, J., 'Myth and Discourse: Myth, Gods, and the Early Written and Iconographic Record.' *Journal of Near Eastern Studies* 50 (1991), 81–105.

Tobin, V. A., 'Mytho-Theology of Ancient Egypt.' *JARCE* 25 (1988), 69–183.

## Chapter 1: Disorder and Creation

Allen, J. P., *Genesis in Egypt: The Philosophy of Ancient Egyptian Creation* (New Haven, 1988).

Assmann, J., *Egyptian Solar Religion in the New Kingdom: Re, Amun and the Crisis of Polytheism* (transl. A. Alcock; London and New York, 1995).

Bickel, S., *La cosmogonie égyptienne: avant le nouvel empire* (Freiburg, 1994).

Borghouts, J. F., 'The Evil Eye of Apophis.' *JEA* 59 (1973), 114–50.

Faulkner, R. O., 'The Bremner-Rhind Papyrus: IV.' *JEA* 24 (1938), 41–53.

Iversen, E., 'The Cosmogony of the Shabaka Text' in S. Israelit-Groll (ed.), *Studies in Egyptology Presented to Miriam Lichtheim*. Vol. 1 ( Jerusalem, 1990), 485–93.

Kemboly, M., *The Question of Evil in Ancient Egypt* (London, 2010).

Mathieu, B., 'Les hommes de larmes: A propos d'un jeu de mots mythique dans les textes de l'ancienne Égypte' in A. Guillaumont, *Hommages à François Daumas*. Vol. II (Montpellier, 1986), 499–509.

Morenz, L. D., 'On the Origin, Name, and Nature of an Ancient Egyptian Anti-God.' *Journal of Near Eastern Studies* 63 (2004), 201–5.

Moret, A., *Le rituel du culte divin journalier en Égypte: d'après les papyrus de Berlin et les textes du temple de Séti Ier, à Abydos* (Genf, 1902).

Saleh, A., 'The So-Called "Primeval Hill" and Other Related Elevations in Ancient Egyptian Mythology.' *Mitteilungen des Deutschen Archäologischen Instituts, Abteilung Kairo* 25 (1969), 110–20.

Sandman-Holmberg, M., *The God Ptah* (Lund, 1946).

Sauneron, S., *Le Temple d'Esna* (5 vols; Cairo, 1959–69).

Schlögl, H. A., *Der Gott Tatenen* (Freiburg, 1980).

Tower Hollis, S., 'Otiose Deities and the Ancient Egyptian Pantheon.' *JARCE* 35 (1998), 61–72.

West, S., 'The Greek Version of the Legend of Tefnut.' *JEA* 55 (1969), 161–83.

## Chapter 2: The Reigns of Kings Re, Shu and Geb

Beinlich, H., *Das Buch vom Fayum: Zum religiösen Eigenverständnis einer ägyptischen Landschaft* (Wiesbaden, 1991).

Fairman, H. W., 'The Myth of Horus at Edfu: I.' *JEA* 21 (1935), 26–36.

Goyon, G., 'Les travaux de Chou et les tribulations de Geb d'après Le Naos 2248 d'Ismaïlia.' *Kemi* 6 (1936), 1–42.

Guilhou, N., 'Myth of the Heavenly Cow' in J. Dieleman and W. Wendrich (eds), *UCLA Encyclopedia of Egyptology* (Los Angeles, 2010), http://digital2.library.ucla.edu/viewItem.do?ark=21198/zz002311pm

Gutbub, A., *Textes Fondamentaux de la théologie de Kom Ombo* (Cairo, 1973).

Hornung, E., *Der ägyptische Mythos von der Himmelskuh: eine Ätiologie des Unvollkommenen* (Freiburg, 1982).

Junker, H., *Die Onurislegende* (Berlin, 1917).

Spiegelberg, W., *Der Ägyptische Mythus vom Sonnenauge, der Papyrus der Tierfabeln, Kufi. Nach dem Leidener demotischen Papyrus I 384* (Strassburg, 1917).

## Chapter 3: The Reign of King Osiris

Caminos, R., 'Another Hieratic Manuscript from the Library of Pwerem Son of Ḳiḳi (Pap. B.M. 10288).' *JEA* 58 (1972), 205–24.

Daumas, F., 'Le sanatorium de Dendara.' *Bulletin de l'Institut français d'archéologie orientale* 56 (1957), 35–57.

Derchain, P. J., *Le Papyrus Salt 825 (B.M. 10051): Rituel pour la conservation de la vie en Égypte* (Brussels, 1965).

Faulkner, R. O., 'The Pregnancy of Isis.' *JEA* 54 (1968), 40–44.

—, 'Coffin Texts Spell 313.' *JEA* 58 (1972), 91–94.

—, '"The Pregnancy of Isis", a Rejoinder.' *JEA* 59 (1973), 218–19.

Gardiner, A. H., *Hieratic Papyri in the BM* (2 vols; London, 1935).

Griffiths, J. G., *Plutarch's De Iside et Osiride* (Cardiff, 1970).

Moret, A., 'La légende d'Osiris à l'époque thébaine d'après l'hymne à Osiris du Louvre.' *Bulletin de l'Institut français d'archéologie orientale* 30 (1931), 725–50.

Osing, J., *Aspects de la culture pharaonique: Quatre leçons au Collège de France (février – mars, 1989)* (Paris, 1992).

Quack, J. F., 'Der pränatale Geschlechts-verkehr von Isis und Osiris sowie eine Notiz zum Alter des Osiris.' *Studien zur altägyptischen Kultur* 32 (2004), 327–32.

Sauneron, S., 'Le rhume d'Anynakhté (Pap. Deir el-Médinéh 36).' *Kemi* 20 (1970), 7–18.

Tower Hollis, S., *The Ancient Egyptian 'Tale of Two Brothers': A mythological, Religious, Literary, and Historico-Political Study* (Oakville, 2008).

Troy, L., 'Have a Nice Day! Some Reflections on the Calendars of Good and Bad Days' in G. Englund (ed.), *The Religion of the Ancient Egyptians: Cognitive Structures and Popular Expressions* (Uppsala, 1989), 127–47.

Yoyotte, J., 'Une notice biographique de roi Osiris.' *Bulletin de l'Institut français d'archéologie orientale* 77 (1977), 145–49.

## Chapter 4: The Reign of King Seth and the Triumph of Horus

Blackman, A. M., and H. W. Fairman, 'The Myth of Horus at Edfu: II. C. The Triumph of Horus over His Enemies: A Sacred Drama.' *JEA* 29 (1943), 2–36

— and —, 'The Myth of Horus at Edfu: II. C. The Triumph of Horus over His Enemies: A Sacred Drama (Concluded).' *JEA* 30 (1944), 5–22.

Broze, M., *Les Aventures d'Horus et Seth dans le Papyrus Chester Beatty I.* (Leuven, 1996).

Colin, M., 'The Barque Sanctuary Project: Further Investigation of a Key Structure in the Egyptian Temple' in Z. Hawass and L. Pinch Brock, *Egyptology at the Dawn of the Twenty-First Century.* Vol. II (Cairo and New York, 2002), 181–86.

De Buck, A., *The Egyptian Coffin Texts.* Vol. I (Chicago, 1935).

Fairman, H. W., 'The Myth of Horus at Edfu: I.' *JEA* 21 (1935), 26–36.

Gardiner, A. H., 'Horus the Behdetite.' *JEA* 30 (1944), 23–60.

Goyon, J., *Le papyrus d'Imouthès fils de Psintaès au Metropolitan Museum of Art de New York (Papyrus MMA 35.9.21)* (New York, 1999).

Griffiths, J. G., *The Conflict of Horus and Seth from Egyptian and Classical Sources* (Liverpool, 1960).

—, '"The Pregnancy of Isis": A Comment.' *JEA* 56 (1970), 194–95.

Kurth, D., 'Über Horus, Isis und Osiris' in Ulrich Luft (ed.), *The Intellectual Heritage of Egypt. Studia Aegyptiaca* 14 (Budapest, 1992), 373–78.

O'Connell, R. H., 'The Emergence of Horus: An Analysis of Coffin Text Spell 148.' *JEA* 69 (1983), 66–87.

Scott, N. E., 'The Metternich Stela.' *Bulletin of the Metropolitan Museum of Art* 9 (1951), 201–17.

Shaw, G. J., *The Pharaoh: Life at Court and on Campaign* (London and New York, 2012).

Smith, M., 'The Reign of Seth' in L. Bareš, F. Coppens and K. Smoláriková (eds), *Egypt in Transition, Social and Religious Development of Egypt in the First Millenium BCE* (Prague, 2010), 396–430.

Swan Hall, E., 'Harpocrates and Other Child Deities in Ancient Egyptian Sculpture.' *JARCE* 14 (1977), 55–58.

## Chapter 5: The Mythic Environment

Allen, J. P. 'The Egyptian Concept of the World' in D. O'Connor and S. Quirke (eds), *Mysterious Lands* (London and Portland, 2003), 23–30.

Fischer, H. G., 'The Cult and Nome of the Goddess Bat.' *JARCE* 1 (1962), 7–18.

Griffiths, J. G., 'Osiris and the Moon in Iconography.' *JEA* 62 (1976), 153–59.

Hornung, E., *The Ancient Egyptian Books of the Afterlife* (transl. D. Lorton; Ithaca, NY, and London, 1999).

Kees, H., *Ancient Egypt: A Cultural Topography* (transl. I. F. D. L. Morrow; London, 1961).

Raven, M. J., 'Magic and Symbolic Aspects of Certain Materials in Ancient Egypt.' *Varia Aegyptiaca* 4 (1989), 237–42.

Ritner, R. K., 'Anubis and the Lunar Disc.' *JEA* 71 (1985), 149–55.

Symons, S., *Ancient Egyptian Astronomy,*

*Timekeeping and Cosmography in the New Kingdom* (Unpublished Doctoral thesis, University of Leicester, 1999).

Wells, R. A., 'The Mythology of Nut and the Birth of Ra.' *Studien zur altägyptischen Kultur* 19 (1992), 305–21.

## Chapter 6: Dealing with the Invisible in Daily Life

Baines, J., 'Practical Religion and Piety.' *JEA* 73 (1987), 79–98.

Dawson, W. R., 'An Oracle Papyrus. B.M. 10335.' *JEA* 11 (1925), 247–48.

Eyre, C. J., 'Belief and the Dead in Pharaonic Egypt' in M. Poo (ed.), *Rethinking Ghosts in World Religions* (Leiden and Boston, 2009), 33–46.

Galán, J. M., 'Amenhotep Son of Hapu as Intermediary Between the People and God' in Z. Hawass and L. Pinch Brock (eds), *Egyptology at the Dawn of the Twenty-First Century*. Vol. II (Cairo and New York, 2003), 221–29.

Lesko, L. H., (ed.), *Pharaoh's Workers, the Villagers of Deir El Medina* (Ithaca, NY, and London, 1994).

Montserrat, D., *Sex and Society in Graeco-Roman Egypt* (London and New York, 1963).

Parker, R. A., *A Saite Oracle Papyrus from Thebes from Thebes in the Brooklyn Museum (P. Brooklyn 47.218.3)* (Providence, 1962).

Quaegebeur, J., *Le dieu egyptien Shai dans la religion et l'onomastique* (Leuven, 1975).

Raven, M. J., *Egyptian Magic* (Cairo and New York, 2012).

Ray, J. D., 'An Inscribed Linen Plea from the Sacred Animal Necropolis, North Saqqara.' *JEA* 91 (2005), 171–79.

Ritner, R. K., 'O. Gardiner 363: A Spell Against Night Terrors.' *JARCE* 27 (1990), 25–41.

—, *The Mechanics of Ancient Egyptian Magical Practice* (Chicago, 1997).

—, 'Household Religion in Ancient Egypt' in J. Bodel and S. M. Olyan (eds), *Household and Family Religion in Antiquity* (Oxford and Malden, 2008), 171–96.

—, 'An Eternal Curse upon the Reader of These Lines (with Apologies to M. Puig)' in P. I. M. Kousoulis (ed.), *Ancient Egyptian Demonology, Studies on the Boundaries between the Demonic and the Divine in Egyptian Magic* (Leuven and Walpole, 2011), 3–24.

Ryholt, K., *The Story of Petese Son of Petetum and Seventy Other Good and Bad Stories (P. Petese)* (Copenhagen, 1999).

Sauneron, S., *The Priests of Ancient Egypt* (Ithaca, NY, and London, 2000).

Szpakowska, K., *Behind Closed Eyes, Dreams and Nightmares in Ancient Egypt* (Swansea, 2003).

—, *Daily Life in Ancient Egypt* (Malden and Oxford, 2008).

—, 'Demons in the Dark: Nightmares and other Nocturnal Enemies in Ancient Egypt' in P. I. M. Kousoulis (ed.), *Ancient Egyptian Demonology, Studies on the Boundaries between the Demonic and the Divine in Egyptian Magic* (Leuven and Walpole, 2011), 63–76.

Teeter, E., *Religion and Ritual in Ancient Egypt* (Cambridge and New York, 2011).

## Chapter 7: The Trials of the Duat (A Guide)

Assmann, J., *Death and Salvation in Ancient Egypt* (transl. D. Lorton; Ithaca and London, 2005).

Kemp, B. J., *How to Read the Egyptian Book of the Dead* (London, 2007; New York, 2008).

Robinson, P., '"As for them who know them, they shall find their paths": Speculations on Ritual Landscapes in the "Book of the Two Ways"' in D. O'Connor and S. Quirke (eds), *Mysterious Lands* (London and Portland, 2003), 139–59.

Spencer, A. J., *Death in Ancient Egypt* (Harmondsworth and New York, 1982).

Taylor, J. H., *Death and the Afterlife in Ancient Egypt* (London and Chicago, 2001).

—, *Journey Through the Afterlife: Ancient Egyptian Book of Dead* (London and Cambridge, MA, 2010).

### Chapter 8: Your Judgment and Life as an *Akh*

Assmann, J., *The Mind of Egypt: History and Meaning in the Time of the Pharaohs* (New York and London, 2002).

—, *Ma'at: Gerechtigkeit und Unsterblichkeit im Alten Ägypten* (München, 2006).

Englund, G., *Akh – une notion religieuse dans l'Égypte pharaonique* (Uppsala, 1978).

Friedman, F., *On the Meaning of Akh (3ḥ) in Egyptian Mortuary Texts* (Ann Arbor, 1983).

Lesko, L. H., 'The Field of Ḥetep in Egyptian Coffin Texts.' *JARCE* 9 (1971–72), 89–101.

### Epilogue: The Myth of Ancient Egypt

Copenhaver, B. P., *Hermetica. The Greek Corpus Hermeticum and the Latin Asclepius in a New English Translation* (Cambridge and New York, 1992).

Jeffreys, D., (ed.), *Views of Ancient Egypt since Napoleon Bonaparte: Imperialism, Colonialism, and Modern Appropriations* (London and Portland, 2003).

McDonald, S., and M. Rice (eds), *Consuming Ancient Egypt* (London, 2003).

Reid, D. M., *Whose Pharaohs? Archaeology, Museums and Egyptian National Identity from Napoleon to World War I* (Berkeley and London, 2002).

Riggs, C., 'Ancient Egypt in the Museum: Concepts and Constructions' in A. B. Lloyd (ed.), *A Companion to Ancient Egypt* (Oxford and Malden, 2010), 1129–53.

## ◀ SOURCES OF QUOTATIONS ▶

PT = Pyramid Text; CT = Coffin Text; BD = Book of the Dead chapter

**Chapter 1 (pp. 17–42) 21** 'The Eight were….'; 'Another of his….' P. Leiden 350 I. Assmann, *Egyptian Solar Religion*, pp. 159, 141; **22, 24** 'knit his fluid….'; 'creator of his….'; 'He is hidden….'; 'expresses his secret….'; 'He began speaking….' P. Leiden 350 I. Allen, *Genesis in Egypt*, pp. 49, 52, 53, 51; **25** 'You took your….' P. Leiden 350 I. Assmann, *Egyptian Solar Religion*, p. 159; **27** 'before two things….' CT 261. Allen, *Genesis in Egypt*, p. 37; **28** 'He completed himself….' P. Leiden 350 I. Assmann, *Egyptian Solar Religion*, p. 141; **28** 'I was alone….' CT 80. Meeks and Favard-Meeks, *Daily Life of the Egyptian Gods*, p. 14; **29** 'I am floating….'; 'Inhale your daughter….' CT 80. ibid., p. 14; **30** 'the remainder' CT 714. Allen, *Genesis in Egypt*, p. 13; **31** 'I made every….' CT 1160. Allen, *Middle Egyptian*, p. 116; **32** 'It is in….' CT 75. ibid., p. 15–16; **32** 'It was through….' CT 714. ibid., p. 13; **32** 'Hail Atum! ….' BD 79. ibid., p. 10; **34** 'I made light….' CT 76. Faulkner, *Coffin Texts*, I, p. 78; **34** 'it is I….' CT 80. ibid., p. 83; **34** 'Atum in his….' BD 17. Adapted from Faulkner, *Book of the Dead*, p. 44; **34** 'goes forth from….' CT 80. ibid., p. 85; **35** 'exercised governance over….' P. Bremner-Rhind. Faulkner, *JEA* 24, p. 41; **35** 'blindness that is….' CT 714. Hornung, *Conceptions of God in Ancient Egypt*, p. 150; **36** 'For it is….' The Teaching for King Merikare, P. Leningrad 1116A, P. Moscow 4658 and P. Carlsberg 6. Simpson *et al. The Literature of Ancient Egypt*, pp. 164–65; **36** 'creator of pasture….'; 'who makes it….' P. Cairo 58038. Assmann, *Egyptian Solar Religion*, pp. 122–23; **37** 'the Roarer' P. Bremner-Rhind 32, 17. Morenz, *Journal of Near Eastern Studies* 63, p. 205; **40** 'the seventieth part….' Plutarch, *Isis and Osiris*. Adapted from Babbitt, *Moralia*, Vol. 5, p. 31; **41–42** 'The Ennead is….'; 'original one who….' P. Leiden 350 I. Allen, *Genesis in Egypt*, p. 51, 52.

**Chapter 2 (pp. 43–66) 44–49** 'more rebellious than….'; 'I have not….'; 'It is not fire….', 'A serpent that….'; 'Heaven pours rain….'; 'Break out, scorpions!….' Mainly from P. Turin 1993 vs. Borghouts, *Ancient Egyptian Magical Texts*, pp. 51, 52, 53, 54; **54** 'He stormed against….'

Edfu Temple, west enclosure wall. Fairman, *JEA* 21, p. 28; **57** 'O eldest god….'; 'their hearts fearful….' The Book of the Heavenly Cow. Lichtheim, *Ancient Egyptian Literature*, II, p. 198; **59–60** 'My body is….'; 'Your baseness be….'; 'It is I….' The Book of the Heavenly Cow. Simpson *et al.*, *The Literature of Ancient Egypt*, pp. 292, 293, 296; **62** 'Moreover, they have….' BD 175. Kemboly, *The Question of Evil in Ancient Egypt*, p. 212; **66** 'its water, its….' The Great Hymn to Osiris, recorded on the Stele of Amenmose. Lichtheim, *Ancient Egyptian Literature*, II, p. 83.

**Chapter 3 (pp. 67–82) 76** 'thrown to the….' PT 532. Allen, *Pyramid Texts*, p. 165; **76** 'felled on his….' PT 478. ibid. p. 279; **78** 'I am Horus….' PT 606. Adapted from ibid., p. 226; **79** 'His sister was….' The Great Hymn to Osiris, Stele of Amenmose. Lichtheim, *Ancient Egyptian Literature*, II, p. 83; **80** 'and Re and….' P. Jumilhac. Tower Hollis, *The Ancient Egyptian 'Tale of Two Brothers'*, p. 196; **82** 'the gods who….' P. Jumilhac. Vandier, *Jumilhac*, p. 126.

**Chapter 4 (pp. 83–108) 83** 'flooded the land….' The Festival of the Two Kites from P. Bremner-Rhind, 5/7. Smith in Bareš, Coppens, and Smoláriková, *Egypt in Transition*, p. 401; **84** 'O evil-doer….' From P. MMA 35.9.21. Smith, *Traversing Eternity*, pp. 156–57. Also see Goyon, *Le papyrus d'Imouthès fils de Psintaês*, p. 86; **85** 'in solitude, his….' The Great Hymn to Osiris, recorded on the Stele of Amenmose. Lichtheim, *Ancient Egyptian Literature*, II, p. 83; **86–91** 'Come to me….'; 'Look my son….'; 'Look, she has….'; 'Horus the Child….'; 'Horus has been….'; 'The crew of….'; 'Thoth, how great….'; 'See, Horus is….'; Papyrus Chester Beatty III, Papyrus Budapest 51.1961, Papyrus British Museum 10059, The Metternich Stele. Borghouts, *Ancient Egyptian Magical Texts*, pp. 3–4, 31, 24–25; **92** 'It is an….' P. Jumilhac. Hollis, *Tale of Two Brothers*, p. 198; **92** 'Horus has been….' PT 535. Allen, *Pyramid Texts*, pp. 102–3; **93–99** 'What is the….'; 'Shouldn't we ascertain….'; 'Award the office….'; 'the rights will….'; 'Are the cattle….'; 'a man's work'; 'Everything that Seth….'; 'Why should my….'; 'As for the….' P. Chester Beatty I. Simpson *et al.*, *The Literature of Ancient Egypt*, pp. 93–101; **100** 'One works magic….'; 'I am Yesterday….' P. Turin 134. Griffiths, *The Conflict of Horus and Seth*, pp. 51, 52; **103** 'disturber suffered hurt….'; 'Abundance is established….' The Great Hymn to Osiris, recorded on the Stele of Amenmose. Lichtheim, *Ancient Egyptian Literature*, II, pp. 84, 85; **102** 'it spreads its….' BD 137A. Faulkner, *Book of the Dead*, p. 127; **105** 'the blood of….' P. Salt 825. Smith in Bareš, Coppens, and Smoláriková, *Egypt in Transition*, p. 412; **105** 'Su mourns, Wenes….' The Rite of Overthrowing Seth and his Confederates, P. Louvre N 3129 and P. BM 10252. Smith in Bareš, Coppens, and Smoláriková, *Egypt in Transition*, p. 413.

**Chapter 5 (pp. 111–40) 114** 'the sky is….' CT 273 (The Cannibal Hymn). Hornung, *Conceptions of God in Ancient Egypt*, p. 131; **115** 'the length of….' CT 80. Allen, *Genesis in Egypt*, p. 22; **116** 'Fine gold does….' British Museum 826 (stele of the brothers Suti and Hor). Adapted from Lichtheim, *Ancient Egyptian Literature*, II, p. 87; **120** 'Don't quarrel with….' The Book of Nut. Symons, *Ancient Egyptian Astronomy*, p. 168; **122** 'you are the….' Stele of Ramesses IV, Egyptian Museum, Cairo JE 48831. Ritner, *JEA* 71, p. 152; **135** 'fresh Nun' The Cairo Calendar (JE 86637). Bakir, *Cairo Calendar*, p. 107; **136** 'no one knows….'; 'who floods the….'; 'no one beats….' The Hymn to Hapy. Lichtheim, *Ancient Egyptian Literature*, I, p. 207, 206, 208; **139** 'Horus cried and….' P. Salt 825. Raven, *Egyptian Magic*, p. 64; **139** 'given to Seth' The Cairo Calendar (Egyptian Museum, Cairo, JE 86637). Bakir, *The Cairo Calendar*, p. 25.

**Chapter 6 (pp. 141–66) 144** 'O people of….' Egyptian Museum, Cairo, JE 44862. Galán in Hawass and Pinch Brock, *Egyptology at the Dawn of the Twenty-First Century*, II, p. 222; **146** The spell to summon Imhotep. P. London 121. See Betz, *The Greek Magical Papyri in*

*Translation*, p. 136; **148** 'If a man….'; 'If a man….'; 'If a man….'; 'If a man….' P. Chester Beatty III. Szpakowska, *Behind Closed Eyes*, pp. 80, 84, 97, 103; **150** 'Retreat, murderers!….' P. Edwin Smith [50] 18, 11–16. Borghouts, *Ancient Egyptian Magical Texts*, p. 15; **151** 'Weeping of Isis….'; 'do not go….' The Cairo Calendar (Egyptian Museum, Cairo, JE 86637). Bakir, *The Cairo Calendar*, pp. 31, 36; **156** 'an [executioner's] blade' Simpson *et al.*, The Tale of the Two Brothers (P. d'Orbiney). *The Literature of Ancient Egypt*, p. 86; **156** 'at the age of….' Ryholt, *The Story of Petese Son of Petetum*, pp. 59, 86; **156** 'prolongs a lifetime….' Hymn to Amun, P. Leiden I 350, chapter 70. Dunand and Zivie-Coche, *Gods and Men in Ancient Egypt*, p. 139; **159–60** 'The sky will….' P. Leiden I 348, verso 2, 5–8. Dunand and Zivie-Coche, *Gods and Men in Ancient Egypt*, p. 127; **160** 'Let these nine[teen]….' P. Leiden I 348. Borghouts, *Ancient Egyptian Magical Texts*, p. 22; **162** 'whose eyes are….' O. Gardner 300, O. Leipzig 42, P. British Museum 10731. ibid. pp. 17–18; **162** 'create strife in….' The Tale of Inaros, P. Krall. Ritner in Kousoulis, *Ancient Egyptian Demonology*, pp. 14–15; **162** 'Appease the spirit….' The Instruction of Ani. Dunand and Zivie-Coche, *Gods and Men in Egypt*, p. 164; **164** 'None comes back….' A Harper's Song (Papyrus Harris 500 and the Tomb of Paatenemheb, Saqqara). Adapted from Lichtheim, *Ancient Egyptian Literature*, I, p. 196; **166** 'This ale of….' P. Hearst [216] 14: 10–13. Borghouts, *Ancient Egyptian Magical Texts*, p. 47.

**Chapter 7 (pp. 169–90) 169** 'You sleep that….' PT 1975B. Hornung, *Conceptions of God in Ancient Egypt*, p. 160; **170** 'that slayer…who….' BD 154. Faulkner, *Book of the Dead*, p. 153; **170** 'Death, the great….' BM 10018. Hornung, *Conceptions of God in Ancient Egypt*, p. 81; **173** 'I arrive at….' BD 17. Kemp, *How to Read the Egyptian Book of the Dead*, p. 33; **176** 'Get back at….' BD 108. Faulkner, *Book of the Dead*, p. 101; **178** 'All-embracing' BD 153B. ibid. p. 152; **179** 'under that sycamore….'; 'Will you live….'; 'the greatest of….' BD 189. ibid. p. 188; **182** 'I am one….' BD 144. ibid. p. 135; **182** 'Mistress of trembling….'; 'Hot of flames….' BD 146. ibid. p. 136; **183** 'it contains spirits….'; 'the spirits who….'; 'cavern sacred to….' BD 149. ibid. p. 139; **184** 'hidden from the'; 'Destruction' BD 149. ibid. p. 144; **186** 'built-up boat of….'; 'What is it?….' BD 99. Adapted from ibid. p. 90–98; **187** 'Get back! Retreat!….' BD 31. ibid. p. 56; **187** 'O *rerek*-snake, take….' BD 33. Taylor, *Journey Through the Afterlife*, p. 186; **188** 'with red ear' PT 1349. Allen, *Pyramid Texts*, p. 173; **188** 'Begone from me….' BD 36. Faulkner, *Book of the Dead*, p. 58.

**Chapter 8 (pp. 191–208) 191** 'We will not….' BD 125. Faulkner, *Book of the Dead*, p. 33; **192** 'Every god you….' A Harper's Song from the tomb of Neferhotep, Luxor. Assmann, *The Mind of Egypt*, p. 170; **193** 'who live on….'; 'O Far-strider who….'; 'O Fire-embracer who….'; 'Do not stand….' BD 125. Faulkner, *Book of the Dead*, pp. 29, 31–32, 27; **195** 'Here I am….' BD 30b. ibid. p. 28; **197** 'Beautiful West' BD17. ibid. p. 44; **198** 'a thousand leagues….' Book of the Dead of Userhat, British Museum EA 10009/3. Taylor, *Journey Through the Afterlife*, p. 255; **203** 'Don't you see….'; 'Take it to….' The Adventures of Setna and Si-Osire, P. British Museum 604. Simpson *et al.*, *The Literature of Ancient Egypt*, pp. 474, 476; **207** 'I am going….' BD 175. Allen, *Genesis in Egypt*, p. 14.

**Epilogue (pp. 209–12) 209** 'A time will….' *Asclepius*, Chapter 24. Copenhaver, *Hermetica*, p. 81; **209** 'Who does not….' Juvenal, 15th Satire. ibid. p. xx.

a = above, b = below, l = left, r = right

**Half title** Detail of the statue of Sesostris I from Lisht, now in the Metropolitan Museum of Art, New York. Drawn by Philip Winton; **Title** Wall painting from the 19th Dynasty tomb of Tawosret in the Valley of the Kings. Photo Richard Harwood; **7** Detail from the Book of the Dead of Nakht. British Museum, London; **8** Late Period cippus. Walters Art Museum, Baltimore; **9** Detail from the Book of the Dead of Userhat. British Museum, London; **12** Undated engraving. Bettmann/Corbis; **18** Detail from the Book of the Dead of Anhai. British Museum, London; **19** Detail from the sarcophagus of Wereshnefer. From *The Metropolitan Museum of Art Bulletin, vol. 9, no. 5*, May 1914; **20** Early 26th Dynasty pyramidion of Wedjahor, possibly from Abydos. The Trustees of the British Museum; **22** Wall painting from the 19th Dynasty tomb of Seti I at Abydos. Photo Jeremy Stafford-Deitsch; **25l** Wall painting from the 18th Dynasty tomb of Horemheb in the Valley of the Kings. Photo Claudia Stubler; **25r** Wall painting from the 20th Dynasty tomb of Montuherkhepeshef in the Valley of the Kings. Photo Tadao Ueno; **27** Wall painting from the 19th Dynasty tomb of Ramesses I in the Valley of the Kings. Francis Dzikowski/akg-images; **29** Wall painting from the 19th Dynasty tomb of Nefertari in the Valley of the Queens. S. Vannini/DeA Picture Library/The Art Archive; **30l** Drawn by Philip Winton; **30r** 26th Dynasty statuette. British Museum, London; **31** Wall painting from the 19th Dynasty tomb of Siptah in the Valley of the Kings. Photo Richard Wilkinson; **33** Detail from the Book of the Dead of Nestanebtasheru. British Museum, London; **37** Wall painting from the 19th Dynasty tomb of Ramesses I in the Valley of the Kings. Francis Dzikowski/akg-images; **39** Wall painting from the 20th Dynasty tomb of Khaemwaset in the Valley of the Queens. Araldo de Luca/The Art Archive; **40** Wall painting from the 20th Dynasty tomb of Tausert (later of Setnakht) in the Valley of the Kings. Photo Wesley Mann; **41** Detail from the Book of the Dead of Ani. British Museum, London; **45** Wall painting from the 19th Dynasty tomb of Nefertari in the Valley of the Queens. Photo Marcelo Romano; **47** Wall painting from the 18th Dynasty tomb of Horemheb in the Valley of the Kings. Photo Yoshiko Ogawa; **48** Wall painting from the 19th Dynasty tomb of Nefertari in the Valley of the Queens. S. Vannini/DeA Picture Library/The Art Archive; **50** Late Period statuette group. Museum of Fine Arts, Budapest; **56** Undated bronze statuette. Williams College Museum of Art, Massachusetts; **59** 18th Dynasty statue. British Museum, London; **61** Drawing of the wall painting from the 19th Dynasty tomb of Seti in the Valley of the Kings. From James Henry Breasted, *A History of the Ancient Egyptians*, 1908; **64** 19th Dynasty relief from the Great Hypostyle hall at Karnak. Werner Forman/Universal Images Group/Getty Images ; **68** Wall painting from the 19th Dynasty tomb of Sennedjem in the Valley of the Kings. Gianni Dagli Orti/The Art Archive; **69** Detail from the Book of the Dead of Hunefer. British Museum, London; **70** Detail from the Book of the Dead of Ani. British Museum, London; **74** Detail from a Graeco-Roman coffin. Metropolitan Museum of Art, New York; **77** Wall painting from the 19th Dynasty tomb of Sennedjem at Deir el-Medina. G. Lovera/DeA Picture Library/The Art Archive; **78** Roman Period scene from the Osiris Chapel in the Temple of Hathor at Dendera. Andrea Jemolo/akg-images; **83** 20th Dynasty statuette. Egyptian Museum, Cairo; **85** Wall painting from the 18th Dynasty tomb of Horemheb in the Valley of the Kings. Photo Richard Wilkinson; **89** Wall painting from the 19th Dynasty tomb of Nefertari in the Valley of the Queens. Photo Brad Miller; **93** Wall painting from the 20th Dynasty tomb of Montuherkhepeshef in the Valley of the Kings. Photo Tadao Ueno; **97** 18th Dynasty statuette. Egyptian Museum, Cairo; **101** Section of the Pyramid Texts inscribed in the Pyramid of Pepi I. Petrie Museum of

Egyptian Archaeology, University College, London; **103** The Shabako Stone, 25th Dynasty. British Museum, London; **107** Wall painting from the 19th Dynasty tomb of Ramesses I in the Valley of the Kings. Andrea Jemolo/akg-images; **112** Detail from the Late Period sarcophagus of Wereshnefer. From *The Metropolitan Museum of Art Bulletin, vol. 9, no. 5*, May 1914; **113** Wall painting from the 19th Dynasty tomb of Nefertari in the Valley of the Queens. S. Vannini/DeA Picture Library/The Art Archive; **114** Roman Period relief from the Temple of Hathor at Dendera. Mountainpix/Shutterstock.com; **117** Detail from the Book of the Dead of Cheritwebeshet. Egyptian Museum, Cairo/Werner Forman Archive; **118** Relief from the Great Palace at Amarna. Egyptian Museum, Cairo; **119** Reconstruction of the Dendera Zodiac from the roof of the Osiris Chapel in the Temple of Hathor at Dendera. Drawn by Dominique Vivant Denon; **120** Wall painting from the 19th Dynasty tomb of Seti in the Valley of the Kings. DeAgostini/SuperStock; **122** Drawing of a wall painting from the temple at Deir el-Bahri. Drawn by Philip Winton; **123** Drawing of a Roman Period scene from the Temple of Hathor at Dendera. Drawn by Philip Winton; **125** Wall painting from the 18th Dynasty tomb of Thutmose III in the Valley of the Kings. Photo Asaf Braverman; **127** Undated statuette. Williams College Museum of Art, Massachusetts; **128** Wall painting from the 18th Dynasty tomb of Thutmose III in the Valley of the Kings. Photo José Acosta; **131** The Nile Delta from space. Jacques Descloitres, MODIS Land Science Team/NASA; **135** 18th Dynasty diadem of Tutankhamun. Egyptian Museum, Cairo; **137** 18th Dynasty statuette. Luxor Museum; **138** 19th Dynasty faience plaque. Egyptian Museum, Cairo; **139** Kochneva Tetyana/Shutterstock.com; **144** 18th Dynasty statue. Egyptian Museum, Cairo; **145** 18th Dynasty ear stela. The Trustees of the British Museum; **146** Late Period statuette. Museum of Fine Arts, Budapest; **147** Wall painting from the 19th Dynasty temple of Seti at Abydos. Photo Garry J. Shaw; **152** 19th Dynasty wooden bust, possibly from Deir el-Medina. Metropolitan Museum of Art, New York; **153** 20th Dynasty stela. Egyptian Museum, Cairo/Gianni Dagli Orti/Corbis; **154** Graeco-Roman statuette. Egyptian Museum, Cairo; **157** Drawn by Philip Winton; **161** 30th Dynasty stela. Metropolitan Museum of Art, New York; **170** Detail from the Book of the Dead of Henutawy. The Trustees of the British Museum; **171** Wall painting from the 18th Dynasty tomb of Tutankhamun in the Valley of the Kings. François Guénet/akg-images; **172** Wall painting from the 19th Dynasty tomb of Irinufer in the Valley of the Kings. Photo Steve Gilmore; **173** Wall painting from the 19th Dynasty tomb of Nefertari in the Valley of the Queens. Photo Jerzy Nowak; **174** 21st Dynasty canopic jars. British Museum, London; **177** Detail from a 12th Dynasty coffin. British Museum, London; **178** Detail from the Book of the Dead of Nesitanebisheru. British Museum, London; **180** Detail from a 21st Dynasty coffin. British Museum, London; **181** Detail from the Book of the Dead of Ani. British Museum, London; **185** Detail from an anonymous the Book of the Dead. British Museum, London; **189a, bl, br** Details from the Book of the Dead of Nakht. British Museum, London; **192** Detail from the Book of the Dead of Iahtesnakht. Universität zu Köln; **193** Detail from the Book of the Dead of Ani. British Museum, London; **194** 17th Dynasty scarab. British Museum, London; **196** Wall painting from the 20th Dynasty tomb of Ramesses VI in the Valley of the Kings. Photo Lien Le; **197** Wall painting from the 19th Dynasty tomb of Nefertari in the Valley of the Queens. DeAgostini/SuperStock; **199** Detail from the Book of the Dead of Anhai. British Museum, London; **200** 19th Dynasty *shabti* statuettes. British Museum, London; **207** Sphinx from Abu Simbel. Roger Wood/Corbis; **208** Matson Photograph Collection/Library of Congress, Washington, D. C.; **210** Colossus from Abu Simbel. Photo Maxime Du Camp; **211** Wall painting from the 18th Dynasty tomb of Nakht in the Valley of the Kings. Metropolitan Museum of Art, New York; **212** Library of Congress, Washington, D.C.